Supercharge Your Communication Skills

Get Your Point Across, Be a Charismatic People
Magnet, and Speak With No Fear.

Jason Forte

Get Ready to Improve all your Conversations & Build Self-Confidence!

✔Five Simple Secrets of Great Communicators. Treat these tips as your bible to improve your communication skills.

✔Free e-book: Stop Limiting Yourself. Expert advice debunks the most common limiting beliefs and forces you to get out of your own head!

✔Printable Small-Talk Field Guide, including conversation topic inventory worksheet. Never be left with nothing to say, and learn to exit a conversation gracefully.

Contents

Introduction

Do you ever look at someone speaking confidently with a group of people and wonder how they manage to communicate so well? You may be similar to this person in so many ways but lacking in this one quality can create a major difference between your experiences and theirs. This is the power of effective communication, and while these skills come more naturally to some than others, they can be learned. This may not come easy for you, but I will introduce simple methods at first and, by the end of this book, you will know exactly what to say and what *not* to say in any situation, and you will understand the reasons why.

Effective communication is at the core of our existence. Without connection, humans would never have been able to multiply and thrive. Critical to connection is our ability to communicate knowledge, thoughts, needs, and feelings. It may seem paradoxical then, that so many of us suffer from a lack of confidence in social settings and find it difficult to connect with others. Whatever the reason behind it, the inability to communicate effectively can hold you back from meaningful connections and limit your exposure to opportunities. On the flip side, by taking small steps toward making your personal interactions more enjoyable and productive, you will quickly see the positive effects of improving your communication skills.

Each chapter of this book will introduce techniques to improve your communication methods one step at a time. You'll start by learning about the various communication styles and which one to use depending on the situation. The hands-on exercises provided in each chapter, along with practical examples, will make it infinitely easier to relate. Moving further, you will learn about the importance of being a good listener and making people feel heard. This is one of the most important aspects of an enjoyable and productive conversation. You will also discover the impact you can have by being empathetic to other people's feelings.

Assertiveness is essential to master if one is to be an effective communicator. This book covers assertive conversational behavior in great detail. Regardless of your communication style in a particular conversation, you can always be assertive while communicating to set healthy boundaries with others. Finally, there's a chapter detailing the art of making small talk interesting. If you suffer from social anxiety or have a disdain for long, awkward silences, then that chapter is for you.

The quick rise of digital communication has opened so many doors, yet brings with it a unique set of challenges. When communicating via written messages, it is easy for misinterpretations and misunderstandings to arise and difficult to smooth them out. Techniques introduced in this book aim to overcome those limitations and teach you to have compelling, clearly worded conversations through text and email.

Overall, effective communication is essential to forming great relationships. People are naturally inclined to help each other out, even more so when they feel connected. Creating connections with other people drives us toward the things we want to achieve in life and exposes us to the things that make our time on this planet more enjoyable. By the end of this book, you will have learned how to tap into your natural strengths and communicate them assertively – not aggressively, not arrogantly, and certainly not meekly – in a manner appropriate to whatever situation you find yourself in.

Chapter 1
Understanding Your Communication Style

"No matter what job you have in life, your success will be determined 5% by your academic credentials, 15% by your professional experiences, and 80% by your communication skills."

Anonymous

Many people think of communication as simply transferring information from one person to another. However, communication is actually much more complex than that. How we deliver our message (our style of communication) can greatly impact how our message is received. To build rapport and feel understood, it is essential that we are aware of our own communication style. Each one of us has a unique way of expressing ourselves, and by learning more about our own inner workings, we can adapt our communication style to better relate to those around us. By understanding our style, we can improve our relationships with others and grow as individuals. Let's take a closer look at what communication styles are and how they can impact our lives.

Why Does Communication Matter So Much, Anyway?

There are many types of communication, from verbal to nonverbal. Verbal communication includes both spoken and written language, while non-verbal communication includes body language and non-verbal cues such as tone of voice and facial expressions. It is important your verbal and nonverbal communications match up with each other. Some communication styles are more effective in a professional or academic setting while they may be useless when dealing with more intimate matters, and vice versa.

Without communication, forming and maintaining any kind of relationship would not be possible. According to Psychologist Robin Dunbar, "language evolved as a way of allowing larger and larger numbers of individuals to live and work together in ever-larger social groups." In other words, language allows us to connect with others and build relationships.

Communication helps us resolve conflicts. If you can express yourself clearly and listen to others openly, it will be easier to find a solution that everyone can be happy with. Effective communication prevents misunderstandings and miscommunications before they begin. When you craft a clear message and take into account how your audience will interpret what you've communicated, you can always say the right thing. Communication helps us build trust. When you communicate effectively with someone, they are more likely to view you as trustworthy, and reliable. They will feel comfortable confiding in you and depending on you. This is especially important in relationships where you need to feel like you can rely on your partner. Trust is also a critical component of teamwork; if team members don't trust each other, they will not be able to work together to achieve maximum results.

Finally, good communication skills are essential for your own happiness. Whether you are looking for a new job, building up your social network, or navigating a family gathering or social function, the ability to communicate effectively will help you attract the kind of people who make you feel comfortable and able to be yourself. People who can clearly articulate their thoughts and ideas are more likely to make a positive impression on those they meet and stand out from the crowd.

Communication Styles

There are several communication styles, and below we focus on the five core ways people express themselves. While each of us encounter and apply all of these styles, they are not all effective. We achieve the best results when we aim to communicate assertively. It is essential to be aware of the communication style you are using in every situation because the way you express yourself will determine the type of response you receive. The same goes for understanding the communication style another person is using. When we identify someone else's poor communication method, we can effectively counter it and keep the conversation productive.

1. Aggressive

The other day I witnessed aggressive communication while buying groceries. I was in the checkout line when the woman in front of me began to argue with the cashier over a coupon. Her coupon was valid for a different item than the one she wished to purchase. The woman began shouting and got angry, and the cashier matched the irate customer's aggressiveness. The situation quickly escalated, and soon the woman was throwing things out of her bag and cursing. The manager got involved, he retrieved the correct item for the coupon given, and diffused the situation. In a way, the woman's bad behavior was rewarded and she got the result she was aiming for.

I'm sure we've all experienced aggressive communication at one point or another - whether it's being on the receiving end of a scathing email or engaging in a heated argument with a loved one. But what exactly is aggressive communication? And why does it tend to escalate conflict rather than resolve it?

Simply put, aggressive communication is any form of communication that is intended to hurt or control another person. Aggressiveness shows no regard for the other person and places the aggressor's needs as the only needs that matter or deserve to be discussed. It can take many different forms, from ignoring to shouting and name-calling, or even making threats or ultimatums. When met with aggression, our natural reaction is to become defensive - which can add fuel to the fire. When on the defensive, a person tends to either submit to the aggressive behavior or confront it with what they believe to be sufficient force to persuade the other person to stand down. A masterful communicator, however, will have the skills and emotional control to de-escalate the situation. He will see the aggression as a weakness, be able to control his emotional response to the behavior, and gain the upper hand.

Aggression can have results but is never a productive way to reach a solution; instead, it usually results in a stand-off or even a physical altercation. Aggressive communication can come across as confrontational, hostile, and belittling. It's important to be aware of how you come across to others and to make sure that your communication style creates an environment where productive dialogue reigns.

In the example above, the customer's aggression showed a lack of respect for the cashier and a failure to inform herself before speaking out. She was wrong but, in her mind, it did not matter. The cashier was offended by the disregard shown to her by the irate customer and responded in kind with aggression, which fanned the flames. The issue was solved once someone assessed the situation, identified the problem, and proposed a solution. There was no compromise and no one sacrificed anything in this situation. The result would have been the same if the communication style had been different, only it would have been solved more quickly and in a much more positive way.

2. Manipulative

Manipulative communication is a way of sending messages that are intended to influence or control the behavior of others. While it can be used to achieve positive outcomes, it can also be used to manipulate and control others. A classic example of manipulative communication can be seen in the movie "The Godfather." In one famous scene, Michael Corleone tries to convince his brother-in-law, Carlo Rizzi, to accept a lucrative offer from the Corleone family. He does this by playing on Carlo's fears and vulnerabilities, making him feel like he has no other choice. It's presented as a great offer he couldn't refuse, but the known meaning of Michael's offer was that Carlo would be killed if he did not accept the terms. This is an extreme example but it clearly demonstrates how manipulative communication can be used to control and influence others.

Manipulative communicators often use deceptive words to exploit the emotions of their listeners to achieve their own goals. They may use flattery or play on someone's insecurities to get them to do what they want. They may also withhold information or lie to maintain control over the situation. Although manipulative communication can be effective in the short term, it typically destroys relationships in the long term. People eventually see through manipulative communicators, earning them an untrustworthy reputation and making it difficult to build lasting relationships.

This communication style is an art, and it can be difficult to detect when manipulation is at play. Guilt trips, being rushed into a decision, intentionally ignoring someone, and playing on a person's insecurities are all good signs of manipulative communication. We run the risk of slipping into a manipulative communication style when we are unable to clearly state our wants or needs. It may be more comfortable to use a manipulative tactic without any bad intentions, but it's always better to be straightforward.

3. Assertive

Assertiveness is a communication style in which a person stands up for their own rights and beliefs while also respecting the rights and beliefs of others. Assertive individuals can express their thoughts and feelings clearly and directly without being aggressive or passive. They are also good at seeking win-win solutions to conflicts.

For example, consider a situation in which you have been assigned a project at work that you do not think you have the time or skills to complete. A passive individual might say yes to the project and then try to figure out how to do it on their own, or they might just do a half-hearted job and hope that no one notices. An aggressive individual might tell their boss that they are not going to do the project, or they might do it but purposely do a poor job. An assertive individual would explain the situation to their boss honestly, state their concerns, and ask for help or additional resources. This assertive approach is more likely to result in a positive outcome for both parties involved.

You may tend to think of assertive communication as being aggressive – many people blur this line. However, the two could not be more different. Assertiveness is a healthy form of communication that involves expressing thoughts and feelings directly, respectfully, and honestly. Assertive communicators are clear about their authentic wants and feel confident in asking for what they need. They also listen attentively to others and respect their opinions, even if they disagree.

Being assertive does not mean being pushy or overbearing. It is about striking a balance between speaking up for yourself and listening to others, placing both sides' priorities at an equal level of importance. Assertive communication is the best way to express yourself in every type of relationship. In personal relationships, assertiveness can help you set boundaries, express your needs and wants, and resolve conflict in a healthy way. In professional relationships, assertiveness can help you build strong working relationships, show your worth, negotiate effectively, and handle difficult conversations. In transactional relationships, assertive communication gets right to the point and expresses respect for the other person while commanding respect in return.

4. Passive

Passive communication is a style of communication where an individual does not express their own wants, needs, or opinions. Instead, they allow other people to control the situation. This can happen in both verbal and nonverbal communication. For example, a passive communicator may not make eye contact, use vague language, or may defer to others when making decisions. While passive communication is not always a bad thing, it can lead to problems if it is used excessively. Individuals who are passive communicators may have difficulty standing up for themselves, which can result in them being taken advantage of by others.

However, by understanding how to recognize and manage passive communication, individuals can learn to use this style of communication more effectively. Being conscious of the words you use when communicating with others is crucial. Avoid using phrases like "I don't know" or "whatever you want to do is fine with me." Not only do these make it seem like you don't have an opinion of your own, but they can also make you seem uninterested in the conversation. The same goes for asking questions. Many passive communicators have the opinion that asking questions may appear to be a sign of weakness. It isn't! When you ask clarifying questions, you show your desire to fully understand

and this gives the other person faith that you are invested in the discussion.

Passive communication can make it difficult to build strong relationships, as it can be seen as a form of avoidance or a lack of interest. Passive communicators frequently assume that others already know what they are thinking or striving toward and place the onus on the other person to understand them better. If you ever get the feeling that your partner, your boss, or a friend or family member doesn't appreciate some of your best qualities, take some time to examine how you communicate with them. Do you make those qualities apparent?

5. Submissive

Submissive communication avoids conflict at any cost. It involves expressing needs and wants in a way that is non-threatening and non-confrontational. For example, instead of saying, "I need you to do the dishes," a submissive communicator might say, "Do you want to help me with the dishes or should I do them on my own?" This approach can be useful on rare occasions, but there is always a better, more assertive way. In a work environment, for instance, a submissive communicator might be less likely to speak up in meetings or confront a coworker about a problem.

While this approach can help if the sole aim is to avoid conflict and move on, there are drawbacks to consistently using a submissive voice. Submissive communicators may have difficulty asserting themselves, and their needs may not be fully heard or met. Speaking submissively communicates to others that you believe your opinions or contributions to be inferior.

Non-Verbal Cues

We all know that communication is about much more than just words. There is also body language, which includes cues like facial expressions, eye contact, posture, and gestures. It turns out that these non-verbal cues can have a big impact on how we interpret what someone is saying. For example, if someone is looking down and away from you while they're talking, they may seem untrustworthy. On the other hand, if they maintain eye contact and have an open posture, they may come across as more credible. In addition, certain facial expressions can convey meaning even when no words are being spoken. A raised eyebrow, for instance, can signal disbelief or skepticism.

1. Body Language

Our body language has a significant impact on what we say. For example, if we are sitting with our arms tightly crossed, we are likely to come across as defensive and uncooperative. On the other hand, if we sit with an open posture, we are more likely to be seen as approachable and trustworthy. Body language can also affect the way we hear others. For instance, if someone is looking directly at us and speaking in a clear voice, we are more likely to pay attention and understand what they are saying. However, if someone is mumbling or averting their gaze, we are less likely to process what they are saying. When standing in a circle of people and a new person seeks to join the conversation, the first way we communicate to them if they are welcome is by our body language. We either open the circle to welcome them in or ignore their presence and display closed body language. The next time you are in a conversation, pay attention to your body language and see how it affects how you communicate.

2. Tone

Everyone has a different way of speaking, and the situation or context often determines that difference. For example, you might speak differently to your boss than you do to your best friend. The tone of your voice can also be affected by your mood - if you're feeling happy, you might speak in a higher pitch, or if you're feeling angry, your voice might be lower and harsher. Your tone can also convey important information about what you're saying. For example, if you're giving someone directions, you will use a different tone than if you were telling them about your day. The tone of your voice can therefore have a significant impact on how your message is received.

3. Emphasizing

When we emphasize, we give certain words or phrases added importance. This can be done for several reasons, but it is often used to express strong emotion or make a point more clearly. Emphasizing can also change the meaning of what we are saying. Thus, emphasizing text can be a powerful tool for both speakers and writers. Used judiciously, it can help add emphasis and clarity to our communication. However, it can also be misused, leading to confusion or even misinterpretation. Therefore, it is important to be careful with what you emphasize and how it comes across.

Emphasizing adds emotion. If you're telling a story, emphasizing certain parts helps paint the full picture. If you're angry, emphasizing words can come off as aggressive.

Emphasis is a powerful way to communicate beyond just the words we are saying; it gives those words extra meaning.

Scenarios

1. Friend at a Cafe vs. Colleagues at Work

When talking to a friend, we generally use a more casual and relaxed communication style. This might involve using slang or colloquialisms, and our body language would be more open and relaxed. In contrast, when talking to our boss or colleagues at work, we generally use a more formal and professional communication style. This might involve avoiding slang and using language that is more precise and to the point. Our body language would also be more controlled and reserved. Ultimately, our communication style depends on the context and who we are talking to.

2. Meeting Aggression

We've likely all been there before. Someone confronts us with a loud tone of voice, animated body language, and frequent interruptions. One way to tackle this is to use a collaborative tone. This means keeping your voice and body language relaxed, making eye contact, and using open-ended questions. For example, if someone interrupted you in the middle of your sentence, you could say something like, "I was just about to explain in detail. Did you have any questions about what I've said so far?". You are being assertive by meeting their interruption with a question. Your question gives the aggressor the validation they seek while you maintain control of the conversation. By asking an open-ended question, you are simultaneously making a small demand of the other person. The aggressive communicator aims to make you question yourself, so if you can turn that around and keep them answering to you, it will be easier to move the conversation in the direction you would like.

It can also be helpful to give them a specific example of what you are discussing. This helps ground the conversation and keeps it from spiraling out of control. For instance, if you're trying to resolve a conflict, you could say something like, "I know we're both upset about what happened yesterday. Let's talk about what went down and how we can move forward from here." By being clear and specific, you can diffuse the tension and come up with a productive solution to continue collaborating.

Staying in Control

Successful communication is always a two-way street. Both parties involved need to be willing to speak openly with each other. It is also important to remember that one cannot ever control another person. The best you can do is guide the conversation and try to stay in control by understanding human psychology at work. Here are a few tips on how to do this:

1. Make Sure You Are Both on the Same Page

It may sound crazy, but make sure you are talking about the same thing. We are constantly bombarded by notifications, many of us have too much on our plate, and it happens that sometimes a conversation starts out of nowhere, each person assuming the other is on their page.

2. Take Turns Speaking and Listening

It is important that both parties feel like they are being heard. Make sure to really listen to what the other person is saying and ask clarifying questions about anything that is not completely clear.

3. Be Aware of Your Body Language and Tone of Voice

Our non-verbal cues can say just as much as our words do, if not more. Make sure you are coming across as open and receptive, or else the conversation will quickly break down.

4. Respect Each Other's Opinions and Boundaries

If you disagree with a point of view, do not put someone down or dismiss their thoughts outright. Communication is about understanding where the other person is coming from, even if you don't see eye to eye.

Following these steps can create a more productive and positive communication experience for everyone involved.

How to Become Aware of Our Communication Style

Have you ever wondered why you hit it off with some people immediately while others just rub you the wrong way? It has a lot to do with communication style. According to research by psychologist David G. Myers, there are four main communication styles: driver, amiable, analytical, and expressive. Consider how you usually communicate with others to figure out your own communication style. Do you tend to be direct and to the point, or are you more laid back and allow others to lead the conversation? Most people tend to gravitate towards one end of the spectrum or the other, and some are more naturally friendly while others are more analytical. Understanding your own communication style can help you to be more aware of how you come across to others and to adjust your communication accordingly. It can also help you better understand those with a different communication style than your own.

Regardless of your communication style, remember that we all communicate in different ways and there is no right or wrong way to communicate. Some people enjoy witty banter and others will shy away from that type of conversation in favor of a more straightforward discussion. Some very quiet people have no problem being assertive; they just choose to express themselves briefly and infrequently. Here are a few tips to help you become more aware of your communication style:

1. Pay attention to the way you communicate with others. Do you tend to talk a lot or be more subdued? Do you use a lot of hand gestures or keep your hands still?

2. Notice how you feel when you are communicating with someone. Do you feel comfortable and confident, or nervous and shy?

3. Think about the types of communication that you prefer. Do you like to have long conversations, or do you prefer shorter exchanges? Do you like to focus on one subject or do you enjoy when a conversation bounces around multiple topics?

4. Ask others for feedback on your communication style. Let them know that you are trying to become more aware of your communication and ask if they have any suggestions on how you can improve.

By becoming more aware of your communication style, you can become a better communicator overall. Be patient with yourself and remember that there is no right or wrong way to communicate - we all just have different styles!

Key Takeaways

- Communication is key in any relationship, whether it be with a friend, family member, coworker, or romantic partner.
- There are many distinct types of communication styles, including aggressive, manipulative, assertive, and passive.
- Communication involves more than just exchanging information - it also includes the way we deliver our message.
- Everyone has a unique communication style, and by understanding our own strengths and weaknesses, we can adapt our communication to better suit the needs of those around us.
- Good communication skills are important because they can help resolve conflicts, build trust, prevent misunderstandings, and make a positive impression on others.

In the next chapter, we'll take a closer look at active listening and how it can help you to be a better communicator by understanding others. We'll also explore some of the common communication barriers and learn how to overcome them.

Chapter 2
Become an Active Listener

"Of all the skills of leadership, listening is the most valuable — and one of the least understood. Most captains of industry listen only sometimes, and they remain ordinary leaders. But a few, the great ones, never stop listening. That's how they get word before anyone else of unseen problems and opportunities."

— Peter Nulty, Fortune Magazine

Listening intently differs from simply hearing someone. Being a good listener is a skill that can only be developed with practice and genuine interest.

You've probably been in this situation before: you want to tell someone something important, but they seem distracted by something else. They seem completely uninterested in what you have to say. They stare into their phones or shift their focus around the room, completely disengaged.

You will absolutely be able to build stronger relationships in both your personal and professional life if you master the art of actively listening to what others say. Not just the words they speak, but the core of what they are trying to communicate. Active listening takes body language, emphasis, and tone of voice into account. It hears what's being said and looks at its deeper meaning.

I want to start helping you communicate more effectively by providing you with a hands-on approach to active listening. You'll find practical examples and simple activities you can practice at work, with family, or at social events.

In this chapter, we will explore the vital function of active listening. It will become clear that listening is the basis for all good conversation. By listening better, we can communicate more effectively and improve our social skills. Finally, you will learn skill-building methods to help improve your active listening skills – even if you are already a great listener.

What Is Active Listening?

Active listening involves focusing on the speaker, taking in what they're saying, processing the information, and responding carefully. Active listening, as opposed to passive listening, is a highly valued interpersonal skill because it ensures that the listener is actively participating in the conversation and can recall key points without repetition.

Active listeners demonstrate and maintain their focus on the speaker by using both verbal and nonverbal cues. This will help you concentrate better and show the speaker that they have your full attention.

Active listeners pay close attention to the speaker, take what they say seriously, and remember the details instead of waiting for their turn and rehearsing their response.

Have you ever been in a situation where you were having a conversation with someone or a group of people, and you were so focused on your contributions, comebacks, or answers that you missed out on what your conversation partner(s) was saying, and when it was your turn to speak, you spoke out of context, or you were asked a question, and you had no answer because you didn't even hear it? Scenarios like this can quickly become uncomfortable and embarrassing, especially if you are trying to make a good impression.

Why Are People Bad Listeners?

Questions like, "Why are so many of us such terrible listeners? Is this a socially learned trait? Were humans always this way?" need to be raised on the path to learning and understanding the art of active listening. Maybe there is a genetic component that came about at some point in time. In such a case, what caused it? The following are some important answers to these questions:

1. The Ability to Process Thoughts More Quickly Than Words

The average person speaks 125 words per minute, but they are cognitively capable of processing 400 words per minute (Lee & Hatesohl, n.d.). This means we have up to 75% more space for "mental chattering." This allows the brain to process additional thoughts while listening, diverting your attention from the speaker.

2. Selective Listening Habits

According to studies, the average person retains only 50% of what is said after 10 minutes, and after a few days, this retention drops by another 50%, leaving the person with only 25% of the complete information (Lee & Hatesohl, n.d.). We pick and choose what information we want to hear and ignore other details of the conversation because most of us are selective listeners.

3. Victims of Listening Barricades

Our conversations frequently contain listening barriers, which is another cause of our poor listening habits. Some obstacles prevent us from paying full attention, such as a lack of interest in the conversation partner's point of view or a simple case of mental fatigue. Now more than ever, we are bombarded by external stimuli from any number of gadgets. A buzzing phone in your pocket could make it hard to focus on the here and now.

4. An Absence of Proper Formal Training

One study shows that, as children move through school, their listening abilities steadily deteriorate. From 90% at the beginning of elementary school to 28% after high school. (Nichols, 1957, cited in Lee & Hatesohl, n.d.). Most of us were never formally taught to listen, we were commanded to listen throughout our younger years. This experience doubtless taught many of us to sit quietly and pretend to pay attention to avoid consequences.

Since very few people have ever been formally instructed on how to listen actively and with intent, we should expect to find ourselves often in the company of people who do not communicate effectively. The truth is most of us learned more about expressing ourselves through written communi-cation during our academic years than any other means of communication or expression. As a result, many of us prefer to talk rather than listen because we have not yet mastered this skill.

Seeing how this skill is somewhat contradictory to today's fast-paced, distraction-driven environment makes it chal-lenging to master. Multi-tasking is, in many circles, valued more highly than shutting out the noise to focus on one person at a time. We live in an environment of information overload and are not always expected to be present. Perhaps more importantly, our brains may not have evolved to be perfect active listening machines. We are social creatures who crave connection, but our listening brain is designed to evaluate input, predict outcomes, form judgments, and perform triage as needed. Active listening forces us to take a slower, more conscious approach to these actions.

Techniques to Become an Active Listener

It takes patience and effort to develop the skill of active listening. It must be developed over time and with a lot of practice. Here are the key techniques that make for great listening skills:

1. Do Not Interrupt

People hate it when they are cut off in the middle of a conversation because it gives them the impression that you do not value or respect their time and opinions. If you think and speak faster than the average person, try slowing down so that others can share their thoughts. Remember, just because there is silence, or a brief break does not mean that you must fill it. Allowing others to finish speaking gives you a much better chance of understanding what they're trying to say.

Interrupting someone, even to respond to what they have just said, may cause the conversation to drift away from the subject at hand.

2. Make Eye Contact

Maintaining eye contact is especially important when listening. This demonstrates to the other person your level of interest in what they have to say. It also shows them that they have your full attention. It is natural for the listener to turn to face the speaker, and it is usually encouraged. However, eye contact can be intimidating, especially for more shy speakers. Make sure you adjust the amount of eye contact depending on who you're speaking to.

3. Use Posture to Show Interest

In interpersonal interactions, posture can reveal a vast amount of information about both parties. When sitting, the attentive listener frequently leans forward or to one side. A small head tilt or simply resting your head on one of your hands could also be signs of engaged listening.

4. Mirroring

Mirroring involves carefully paraphrasing or repeating what your conversation partner(s) has said to show you understand what they have said. Reflection is a crucial skill that can be applied to support the speaker's point. This could come in the form of a question, as if you are clarifying you understood them correctly, or as a statement to emphasize a point they've made that you find intriguing.

5. Pay Attention to Nonverbal Signs as Well

What someone is attempting to say can be communicated just as effectively through facial expressions, tone of voice, and mannerisms as it can through words. Learn to read the other person's facial expressions and gestures, such as whether their smile looks genuine or if their arms are crossed angrily or in a relaxed way. Even over the phone, a person's tone can convey a lot about their current mental state, whether they appear irritated or placid, bored or eager to hear more.

When someone's nonverbal cues do not match up with what they are telling you, it is important to determine the reason. Some people have natural communication barriers and it will help you to know that; others may be attempting to deceive you.

6. Communicate with Facial Expressions

The automatic reflection of the speaker's facial expressions is an indication of attentive listening as you show your own emotions via facial expressions. These thoughtful gestures can help express sympathy and understanding in highly emotional situations. Although, when someone makes a conscious effort to mimic another person's facial expressions rather than simply reflecting them, it is an indication of inattention.

7. Maintain a Flexible Mindset

Simply listen without passing judgment, making mental notes to criticize, or coming up with solutions. You derail your ability to listen attentively when you allow yourself to be sidetracked by inner chatter.

Make no assumptions when listening. Remember that the other person merely uses words to express the emotions and ideas flowing through their mind, and none of us express ourselves perfectly. Only by listening and asking questions can you learn what they are thinking and feeling.

8. Remember Details

The human mind's ability to remember details over time is notoriously poor. Recall a few key points to demonstrate that the speaker's messages have been heard and understood. Recalling specifics, thoughts, and ideas from previous conversations shows that you paid attention, which will likely encourage the speaker to continue.

9. Clarify and Ask Questions

Clarification entails requesting that the speaker confirm the intended meaning is understood. Sometimes questions with no right or wrong answers are asked so that the speaker can elaborate on a point that they believe requires more explanation. Demonstrate your listening skills by asking thoughtful follow-up questions and making interesting comments that clarify or expand on the speaker's points.

To reiterate a vital point: never assume you understand, make *certain* you understand! It's not always easy to formulate an open-ended question on the spot. Let's say something is unclear or it rubs you the wrong way. Try repeating the person's statement back to them, this time in the form of a question. For example, you turn in a report and as your boss is flipping through it, she says "this is no good". You could assume she meant your whole report is unusable and her way of saying so was rude. Or you can respond "this is no good?" in a neutral, inquisitive tone. She will then be naturally compelled to elaborate on what exactly is no good. Maybe an issue you've brought up is no good for the company and she is thrilled you discovered it. Perhaps she's found a typo or incorrect statement. By simply repeating her words back, you open the door to dialogue that will give you plenty of information. This is a powerful tactic, and we will discuss it in more detail in the Negotiations chapter.

10. Summarize

You, the listener, should use this technique by repeating what your conversation partner said in your own words back to them. Reiterating the main ideas of the speech in a clear, logical manner allows the speaker to make any necessary corrections.

11. Do Not Force Your Ideas or Solutions

Giving someone your undivided attention and encouragement instead of advice or instructions may be more satisfying. When a friend is suffering from health problems, they are more likely to want to share their feelings with you and rant rather than receive a slew of instructions on what they should do.

The majority of people would rather solve their own problems. When you must present an excellent idea, first determine whether they are interested in hearing it. For example, you may ask, "Are you willing to hear my ideas?"

12. Eliminate Distraction

You should avoid getting distracted in any way if you want to be an active listener. Fidgeting, looking at your watch or around the room, checking your phone, a lack of eye contact, and doodling are some examples.

The Importance of Active Listening

Active listening is necessary for all aspects of life to run more smoothly. Individuals will feel more comfortable sharing their thoughts and feelings with you if you improve your listening and comprehension skills. You'll learn how to resolve conflicts and improve your interpersonal relationships. Your job performance would also improve because you would be better at understanding tasks and meeting your objectives.

The following are just a few of the many situations in which active listening can be beneficial:

1. In Your Relationships

When you master the skill of active listening, you begin to understand the other person's point of view better and your responses become more empathic. This is essential when communicating with a spouse, child, sibling, parents, or friend to maintain a healthy relationship.

As an active listener, you gain respect because you learn to prioritize the needs and feelings of others over your own. This implies that the other person is the primary focus during a conversation. Don't focus solely on yourself, especially if your conversation partner is experiencing emotional distress.

When speaking with a loved one, friend, or family member, they are frequently looking for an opportunity to vent and simply want to be heard. As a result, developing the ability to listen and remain silent when necessary is a crucial skill. You should always know when to refrain from making comments, throwing around criticisms, and providing solutions when they are not necessary.

2. In a Work Setting

Do you ever feel socially awkward at work? If so, you're in good company. By listening actively in office conversation, you place the focus on others while appearing more comfortable as a result.

Not sure how to get along with your boss? By consistently using active listening you will appear more dependable and competent, and the result of this is not merely superficial – you will begin performing better because you fully understand the assignment and its purpose. Listening actively by asking clarifying questions and staying focused inspires others to have confidence in you while giving you the information you need to succeed.

This powerful tool for communication will help you understand the challenges at work and collaborate better with others to find solutions.

3. In Social Gatherings

Active listening is necessary for successful social interaction because it allows you to focus on the other person while also ensuring that you fully comprehend what they are saying and can contribute meaningfully to the conversation.

It can be used to ask open-ended questions that demonstrate that you are listening, evaluating, and seeking additional information. All of these elements help individuals make new connections.

Someone suffering from social anxiety may find it difficult to initiate a conversation with you, but if you employ your attentive listening skills, it can help them break out of their shell and gain confidence in their ability to hold a conversation.

If we flip that around, let's say you struggle with social anxiety. You may not feel comfortable interjecting in a group setting. But if you find yourself on the outskirts of a group of people discussing a topic you're interested in, the surest way to get involved is by asking a thoughtful question. Your question will likely be met with an answer you can respond to. Even if you have nothing else to say, you will have made an impression simply by contributing a well-considered question, as opposed to staying silent or barging in with an off-topic statement.

In short, active listening – specifically asking questions – makes you appear more interesting, confident, and enjoyable to be around. Active listening perpetuates effective communication. Listen actively, pose a simple, well-worded question, and listen intently to the response. People enjoy being asked about themselves or a topic in which they are interested.

Ways to Improve Active Listening

We've all encountered situations in which our "listeners" were distracted or uninterested. Perhaps you want to improve your own active listening skills so that you don't do the same thing to others.

Here are a few tips for becoming a better active listener and encouraging others to do the same:

1. Develop Your Own Interest in the Subject

To become more interested in learning about anything, simply be curious about it. You'll find yourself asking more questions to comprehend what the other person is saying.

2. Find a Subject That Both of You Are Interested In

Small talk is an excellent way to break the ice and learn more about someone. It is easier to keep a conversation going if you and the other person are both interested in the same thing.

3. Improve Your Listening Skills

Active listening takes time and effort to develop, just like any other skill. Take your time and be gentle with yourself as you learn. Maintaining these skills, perhaps even mentioning them, could inspire the person with whom you're interacting to follow in your footsteps. When you say something like "I am putting my phone away so I'm fully focused on you right now," the other person will likely feel respected and important. Most people will act in kind to make sure you feel respected and important as well.

Know When It Is Appropriate to Leave a Conversation

Knowing how and when to gracefully leave a conversation can be stressful. Excuse yourself too early and you may appear rude or disinterested; stick around too long and people will become uncomfortable. There is an ebb and flow to conversation, so a quiet moment does not always indicate the need to exit. People generally look down or around the group while coming up with a change of subject.

Observe the body language of those around you. Are they looking around the room? Does their body language appear as if they are pulling themselves away from the conversation? Are they saying they need to go? If so, it's time to excuse yourself as well.

Key Takeaways

- You cannot become a good communicator without active listening skills
- Listen adequately before speaking to enhance your conversations
- The non-verbal cues from your speaker or communication partner are just as important as their verbal cues.
- Active listening boosts your likability and attracts people to you.

Being an active listener will make you connect with people on a deeper level. Active listening entails more than just hearing someone's words; it also entails comprehending their message and empathizing with them. It makes one a better friend, coworker, and spouse.

If you want to improve your communication skills, you should try active listening. It may take a little practice, but it's worth it.

This next chapter will emphasize a key skill in active listening: empathy and validation. This skill will help you relate to others better and vastly improve your communication skills and likability in the long run.

Chapter 3
Learning Empathy and Validation

"When we listen, we hear someone into existence."

— Laurie Buchanan, PhD

Practicing empathy and validation in our daily interactions with others will go a long way toward strengthening our relationships. Validation is all about learning to recognize how someone feels, accepting their emotions, and refraining from judgment when it comes to their thoughts and behaviors.

Listening with intent, to understand the message being conveyed, is an example of empathic listening. Not only must you put yourself in the other person's shoes, but you must also try to comprehend what they went through. You must ask yourself, "If I were in this situation, what might I have done?" It doesn't matter if they're right or wrong;

empathy is to try and understand the feelings they're experiencing.

Validation in this context would be to acknowledge the other person's feelings and recognize they deserve a place in the conversation – that they are valid emotions. It is not about analyzing the feelings or agreeing on whether they are right or wrong. Validating comes from a place of neutrality and respect, and it merely communicates that you respect the existence of the other person's opinion or contribution to the conversation. It is the opposite of ignoring or bulldozing the other person.

Imagine you've been thinking up a great solution to a problem at work for the past two weeks. You go into your team meeting nervous but excited to pitch the idea to your colleagues. It's your turn to speak, you give your presentation and it's met with crickets. No one has any questions, facial expressions around the room are blank, and the conversation moves on to the next topic. Or let's say you have told your significant other that something they do upsets you, only to have them roll their eyes and walk away without responding. These are examples of invalidation in communication.

We all need validation in some form or another. Most people struggle to communicate things that make them feel vulnerable, and when they do offer up a sensitive piece of personal information, the listener must validate it.

Our natural urge for self-preservation interferes with our ability to speak openly about the things that matter most.

Direct statements like, "It makes me jealous when you do that because it triggers x insecurity," or "You left me out and that makes me feel like a bullied kid on the playground," might lead to a heartfelt conversation, but could also lead to ridicule. As such, shame and fear usually keep our darker feelings locked away in the dungeon of our minds. We tend to speak in circles around them and, when the listener fails to understand or makes light of the issue, we may become frustrated and angry because we do not feel seen. Hence, we must express our feelings clearly and assertively.

When a person experiences empathy, they feel comfortable opening up and sharing things that give a conversation more meaning. Once a person opens up, it is important to feel like what they have shared is validated and respected by the listener. Without empathy and validation, effective communication cannot be achieved. If you are attempting to improve communication with someone in your life who invalidates you, it will be an uphill battle.

Handling Someone Who Invalidates You

The way someone treats you reflects how much they value you. The experience of being invalidated can be excruciatingly painful, even unbelievable, especially when it comes from an unexpected person.

Even if your life is filled with wonderful people, there are bound to be times when you do not feel validated. The easiest example of this would be a nasty argument with someone who interrupts, ignores you, and belittles the points you raise. Invalidation can also appear innocuous, however, and be expressed in ways that at first seemed caring.

Assertive communication is critical when confronting someone who does not validate you. The suggestions below will help when dealing with being invalidated:

Calculated Reactions

When someone invalidates your feelings, you may be tempted to lash out. When responding to invalidation, consider the consequences of whatever action or words you intend to use. Before responding, ask yourself, *"What do I stand to gain from this outburst," "Does their opinion affect me?"*

The reason it's so important to validate others is that it is maddening to be disregarded. Rather than react angrily to this type of disrespect, think of your goal for the conversation and try to maintain focus on that end result. Don't get sidetracked.

Stick to Your Point

Some people might attempt to empathize but want you to look at your situation from their perspective, ignoring your feelings and accepting their judgment.

When you try to express your feelings to them, they may find it difficult to understand. Say something like, "I know what you're thinking, but I just want you to hear me out on this one." When you point this out to them, they may respond positively. You didn't let them dominate the conversation with their point of view but instead demanded they at least listen to what you have to say.

Define Boundaries

When someone invalidates you, they tell you your feelings are incorrect and insignificant. Even when you try to show empathy, you may discover that it hurts you even more. They somehow end up playing the victim and say you only care about yourself.

They can make you feel bad, but instead of saying, "I know I made you angry, and I'm sorry," they say, "You're so annoying to get upset over such a minor issue."

Avoid people who display manipulative behavior. Do not let them tell you what is right or wrong. You must maintain your distance so that they do not judge you or make you doubt yourself. You may not be able to avoid them entirely, but make sure to limit their influence over your life and your choices. Spending time with manipulators makes it impossible to form your authentic identity.

Deal with It

If you've been invalidated several times and don't like how things are going because you're unsure and don't believe the person is doing it on purpose, confront them about it. Some people intentionally invalidate you, while others do so unknowingly. Calling someone out and having a conversation with them about the issue is sometimes the best course of action.

Bringing these issues to light may cause the other person to feel guilty, resulting in a change in how they respond to your questions and listen to you. They may express regret for dismissing your feelings in the past and inquire whether you are still on good terms with them while also thanking you for your understanding.

If the people who invalidated you were aware of what they were doing, there is a chance that they could change their behavior. Say something calm like, "I know we think differently, but do you realize how much you hurt my feelings?" or, "This relationship can't be equal if you ignore my emotions." Then, they may go on to explain why they initially ignored you, or they may simply apologize immediately after you have brought them to the realization.

Prepare for Invalidation

Allowing for disappointment may help you feel less pain or recover faster from invalidation, which can occur at any time, intentionally or unintentionally. You might not even feel anything because you were prepared for the worst. When conversing or arguing, be prepared for veiled invalidating phrases like "Just accept your flaws; we all have one" and "Try not to see everyone as your enemies; we are just telling you the truth."

Why Choose Empathy and Validation?

Invalidation can lead to self-doubt. Empathy is at the heart of healthy relationships and effective communication.

Validating someone shows you care about their feelings and are willing to place theirs as equal to yours to reach a conclusion that benefits both of you. You may not agree with what they think but you respect their feelings. This creates a productive dynamic of mutual respect and trust. Once you have made the effort to understand another point of view, you have free reign to disagree, and you have earned the right to propose your own approach.

Everyone has a unique point of view, which influences their behavior. Their actions may be correct or incorrect depending on how they see things. Validating their feelings will make them appreciate you, understand your reasoning, and want to hear your opinions on certain issues. Empathizing with others makes them feel more at ease around you. It also strengthens relationships.

Ways to Demonstrate Empathy

Active Listening

People appreciate having someone they can always talk to and who will hear them out. It's reassuring to know that you have someone to turn to when you're facing a difficult situation, someone who will listen to you without passing judgment.

Actively listen to determine what the person is saying and ask clarifying questions to ensure that what you understood is correct. Listen with the intention of fully comprehending what the speaker is saying; don't assume you understand.

Allow them to speak freely, and try to keep a non-judgmental attitude. The goal is to take everyone at face value and give them the benefit of the doubt, allowing them to express themselves fully.

Positively Associate

When you surround yourself with people who are willing to listen to your thoughts and care about your feelings, you will find yourself doing the same. It's easier to reciprocate actions and feelings expressed to you.

A supportive social circle will validate your emotions, boost your self-esteem, and be honest with you when you have a misguided perspective on things. They motivate you to validate others and actively listen to others. Even when they are preoccupied with their own problems, they make time for you.

Be Genuine

Make people feel at ease around you before you begin a conversation. Ask how they're doing and joke around. Build rapport. Say things like "How are you?" and "I haven't seen you in a long time." When they're calm around you, they'll open up and see that you care.

Don't Jump to Conclusions

Put aside everything you already know about a subject while listening to other people's perspectives. Try to understand their perspective and guide them without criticism. Listen to them with an open and sincere heart. No one's life is like yours, and you don't expect other people to have gone through the same things you have in their own lives. Some people are going through more than they appear, and they don't need someone to blame or criticize them without knowing why.

Do not compare their lives to yours or someone else's. Empathic listening focuses on the person talking and does not seek to relativize their experience.

Acknowledge Feelings

It is not always necessary to offer advice or alter a person's viewpoint when they converse with you. They need someone to listen to and understand them. They only need a shoulder to cry on to relieve the stress.

Try to acknowledge that they have feelings and are important. Instead of saying things like "I completely understand how you feel" or "Everything happens for a reason," try to empathize with them. Tell them things like, "I'm so sorry this is happening to you," and "I can't imagine how you're feeling."

Recognize that they see things differently and they have the right to express their emotions. You can share a similar experience with them to help them relax, confide in you, and let go of their burden.

Experience Their Lives

Unless you have firsthand experience, you may not be able to truly understand and empathize with someone. You should try to put yourself in the shoes of others. Examine the challenges they face, their reactions to those challenges, and the external forces present in their life.

Show Physical Attention

Physical attention, when used appropriately, can be a wonderful way to communicate empathy. This can come in the form of a favor, like cooking or doing a chore for someone. It could be writing a note or sending a gift. It could also be a hug or a squeeze of the shoulder. Unlike verbal ways of communicating, physical touch can easily cross a boundary and make someone feel uncomfortable. Some of us would prefer a long hug to words of reassurance. Others may feel awkward or violated if, in the middle of venting, they suddenly found themselves smothered in the arms of the listener.

How does it feel when you receive physical attention? Do you enjoy getting hugged by a friend or colleague? Are you happy when someone sends you flowers or buys you a coffee when you're having a bad day? Or would you prefer to have more of a defined boundary between these types of displays of affection? Some people crave physical attention – it feels uplifting and makes them feel secure. Others object to their physical space being invaded and it can feel threatening.

Sometimes our physical presence is enough to make someone feel good, other times someone may need to be left alone. If you get mixed signals from someone, it's good practice to ask if they need some space. If you feel like a physical show of support may be appropriate, first communicate! Just ask a question like "Can I give you a hug?" to confirm the other person is comfortable.

If someone declines physical attention, don't question their reasoning, and don't take offense. This is simply a boundary of theirs that likely has nothing to do with you.

The same goes for you. If you have strong boundaries when it comes to your physical space, it is important to assert how you prefer to be treated. Let's say you don't like to be hugged, yet you have a colleague that tends to throw her arms around you at work when something good happens. You should be able to express this simple boundary without the need to explain. A statement like, "I don't like being hugged," should be met with validation. You don't need to explain further, nor do you need to take responsibility if that makes the other person feel awkward.

Key Takeaways

- Actively listen to others and validate their feelings.
- Don't settle for less when you're worth more.
- Treat people fairly.
- Use active listening and cues to determine how you should display empathy in a given situation.
- Speak up if someone displays empathy to you in a way that makes you uncomfortable.

Everyone has emotions, and we must recognize them. We must give others the opportunity to be heard, seen, and loved. We must show respect by allowing others to speak and express themselves. If you believe that a person is being honest with you, it is important to validate their feelings by empathizing with them. Investigate what they are saying and try to understand where they are coming from. Validation is a two-way street, so you should expect this treatment from the people around you as well. Once we understand how to make others feel respected and comfortable, the conversation becomes easier and more productive. By learning about the other person, you gain the tools you need to communicate with them effectively.

Chapter 4
Master the Art of Assertiveness

"Staying silent is like a slow-growing cancer to the soul... There is nothing intelligent about not standing up for yourself. You may not win every battle. However, everyone will at least know what you stood for—YOU."

— Shannon L. Alder

Assertiveness is the key to effective communication and people skills, yet it is frequently misunderstood. We tend to view assertiveness as standing up for ourselves, but it's a much more versatile skill. It can be as simple as deciding what's for dinner, or it can be as intense as negotiating a fair salary or drawing a strict boundary with a family member.

Learning to be assertive is an essential skill for success and happiness. It might take some getting used to if you're not used to flexing that muscle, but this chapter will help with that.

What Is Assertiveness?

Assertiveness is the ability to state your opinions and stand up for yourself in a respectful way without offending others or becoming aggressive.

When you're assertive, you can clearly and confidently express yourself. You can also listen to others and respect their point of view, even if you don't agree. It's the ability to have a back-and-forth conversation without getting defensive or putting your own needs aside.

Nice Person Dilemma

Warren Buffet once said, *"The difference between successful people and really successful people is that really successful people say no to almost everything."*

Many people struggle with being assertive because they don't want to be seen as pushy, bossy, or difficult. They've been taught that it's necessary to be a "nice person," and being assertive seems to go against that.

Being assertive doesn't mean being rude, aggressive, or selfish. It's simply a way to express yourself honestly and confidently while respecting the needs of everyone else.

For example, let's say you're out to dinner with a group of friends, and the bill comes. One of your friends tried to split it evenly, even though you only had a salad and water, while they ordered an entree, appetizer, and dessert. An assertive person would politely say, "I only had a salad, so I'll Venmo you for my share."

On the other hand, a passive person might not say anything and just Venmo their friend the full amount, even though they know it's not fair. An aggressive person might say something like, "You're such a cheapskate! I can't believe you would try to make me pay for your whole meal!"

Both the passive and aggressive responses would likely cause tension and conflict, whereas the assertive response is direct and respectful.

Why Being Assertive Is Important

Being assertive is important for both your personal and professional life. In your personal life, assertiveness can help you set boundaries, express your needs, and stand up for yourself. You will feel free because you are able to express yourself. For example, if you're feeling overwhelmed by your friend's constant texting, you can be assertive and say, "I need some space; I'm going to turn my phone off for a few hours."

In your professional life, assertiveness can help you feel more confident in your abilities, build better relationships with your co-workers, and advocate for yourself regarding salaries and promotions.

For example, let's say your boss asks you to work on a new project that would give you experience that will move you further in your career. You want to volunteer but are worried you won't be able to dedicate enough time to the project. An assertive person would say something like, "I'm interested in the project, but I'm not sure I can take it on with my current workload. Can we have a look at where I should prioritize?"

That way, you're expressing your interest in the project while also being honest about your current workload. This will start a conversation about managing your time rather than blindly agreeing to take on more work. One simple sentence told your boss that you're eager for new opportunities, you take your current role seriously, and you can be depended on because you manage your time well.

On the other hand, a passive person might not say anything and just agree to take on the project, even though they're already overwhelmed. An aggressive person might say something like, "I don't have time for this! You need to find someone else."

When you're assertive, you can express yourself clearly and confidently without getting flustered or apologizing for your thoughts and opinions – or worse, never speaking up at all. Even when you don't agree, you can listen to others and respect their point of view. This is the ability to have a back-and-forth conversation without getting defensive or putting your own needs aside. People know where you stand and they feel they can trust you.

The Benefits of Being Assertive

The benefits of assertive communication are numerous.

When you're assertive, you can clearly express your needs and boundaries. This helps prevent misunderstandings and conflict in your relationships. When conflict arises, assertiveness can help you productively and respectfully resolve it before it spirals out of control or becomes something bigger than it should be.

Being assertive will also help boost your confidence and self-esteem. When you're able to express your thoughts and opinions without apology or hesitation, it can help you feel more confident and validate your own opinions and feelings. This can lead to positive changes in your life, like taking on new challenges and speaking up for yourself more often.

You project an image of reliability and trustworthiness. People gravitate toward assertive people who are known for speaking their minds. An assertive person says 'no' when they're unable to commit to something, so their 'yes' is powerful; they can be counted on to follow through. An assertive person doesn't agree just to go with the flow, so people know their opinion is authentic.

Finally, assertiveness can help reduce stress and anxiety. When you can clearly communicate your needs, you're less likely to worry about what others think or whether you're too "needy." This can help you feel more relaxed and confident in your interactions with others. You will ensure your needs are met when you clearly communicate them.

Be Assertive, Not Aggressive

It's important to remember that there is a difference between being assertive and being aggressive. Assertiveness should not be used to bully or steamroll others.

When you're aggressive, you tend to dismiss others and their opinions. You might interrupt people or use hostile or threatening language when they're speaking. This kind of communication style can damage your relationships and make it difficult to resolve conflict productively. It certainly does not open the door to effective communication.

On the other hand, when you're too passive, you might avoid conflict altogether or allow others to walk all over you. You might agree to things even when you don't want to or apologize for your thoughts and opinions. This can lead you to resentment and feeling powerless in your relationships.

The goal is to find a balance between the two extremes. When you're assertive, you can express your thoughts and opinions without being aggressive or passive. You can have a back-and-forth conversation without getting defensive or putting your own needs aside. In a way, to be assertive is to be neutral. You value your opinion enough to bring it to the conversation, and you value the opinions of others enough to weigh them equally to yours. No one needs to agree or disagree with your opinion; it's simply your opinion and it deserves to be there.

When you are assertive, you are confident and clear in your communication. You state your needs and wants without being disrespectful or making demands of others. You do not push your opinion as truth. On the other hand, being aggressive means being forceful and demanding. You might shout or make threats to get what you want. You pressure others to see your side and you disregard or ignore theirs. This kind of behavior creates conflict and puts people on the defensive until they stop listening altogether.

How to Be More Assertive

If you're not used to speaking up for yourself, it can be tough to know how to start. Here are a few tips for being more assertive in your communication style:

Use "I" and Avoid "You" Statements

Making statements that begin with "I" can help you take ownership of your thoughts and opinions. For example, instead of saying, "You never listen to me," you could say, "I feel like I'm not being heard."

Similarly, avoid using "you" statements when possible. These tend to sound accusatory and can put people on the defensive. For example, instead of saying, "You're being really selfish," try, "I'm feeling overwhelmed and need some help."

When you make "you" statements, it can sound like you're placing blame on the other person. For example, instead of saying, "You're always interrupting me," you could say, "I need some time to finish what I'm saying."

This can help the conversation feel less like a blame game and more like a productive discussion. It also allows you to state your needs without making demands of the other person. By consistently focusing on what you need rather than what someone else fails to provide, your mindset is likely to adopt a more positive outlook and you'll feel like you have more control over all the situations in your life.

Practice Active Listening

Active listening and assertive communication go hand in hand. When you truly listen to what someone is telling you, you can assert yourself in a meaningful way.

For example, you might say something like, "I understand that you're feeling frustrated because you feel like your voice isn't being heard. Is that right?"

This shows that you not only listened to the other person, but you empathized to understand their feelings. It can also help diffuse a tense or emotional situation.

Be Clear

When you use vague phrases or talk in circles around a subject, it can lead to miscommunication and conflict. For example, you might assume that the other person knows your feelings or needs while they have no idea what you are trying to convey.

It's important to state your needs directly. For example, instead of saying, "You should know that I'm feeling upset," you could say, "I'm feeling upset right now, and here's why."

You have communicated how you feel and what you need; you have not left anything up for interpretation. Simply stating "I'm upset," can cause the other person to assume many things but since you added the slightest bit of clarification, everyone can feel at ease. Being clear like this can help you avoid misunderstandings and ensure that your needs are being met while remaining pleasant to be around even when you're not feeling your best.

Set Boundaries

Boundaries in your relationships are critical! This means knowing what you're comfortable with and what you're not willing to accept. Through boundaries, we express our self-worth and safeguard our wants and needs.

For example, you might need to set a boundary with a friend who always wants to vent about their problems. You might tell them that you're happy to listen, but you need to limit the conversation to 10 minutes. You might need to set a boundary with a family member who is always asking for money. You might tell them that you're not able to lend them money at this time.

Setting boundaries can be tough but doing what's best for you is essential. This can help protect your own emotional well-being while still being supportive of the other person.

Know Your Limits

It's also important to know your limits. This means knowing when you need to take a break or walk away from a situation.

For example, you might need to take a break from a conversation that's starting to feel overwhelming. You might say something like, "I need a minute to collect my thoughts. I'll be right back."

You might need to walk away from a situation if it gets too heated. You might say, "I'm not going to continue this conversation if we keep yelling at each other. I'm going to take a walk, and we can talk when we've both calmed down."

Knowing your limits can help prevent you from getting overwhelmed or feeling like you're in over your head.

Avoid Apologizing Unnecessarily

When you apologize unnecessarily, it can make you seem like you're not confident in what you're saying. For example, you might say, "I'm sorry, but I think you're wrong."

Instead of apologizing, you can simply state your opinion. For example, you might say, "I understand what you said but I see this very differently."

You will sound more confident and avoid getting into a back-and-forth argument. Apologize when you have done something wrong, not for having an opinion.

Speak Up for Yourself

It's important to speak up for yourself, even if it means disagreeing with someone else. For example, you might need to tell your boss that you don't agree with their decision.

You might need to tell a friend that you don't appreciate being ignored.

Standing up for yourself can be tough but doing what's best for you is important. This can help you build your self-confidence and prevent you from being taken advantage of.

Social Anxieties and Assertiveness

It is quite common to feel anxious in social situations, so you are not alone if this applies to you. Harvard Medical School research suggests that up to 12.1% of US adults suffer from some form of social anxiety. One of the main symptoms of social anxiety is a fear of negative evaluation from others. This can manifest itself in several ways, such as feeling self-conscious, obsessing over what others think of you, or feeling like you are being judged.

These fears can make it difficult to assert yourself in social situations. You may avoid speaking up or expressing your opinion for fear of being judged or criticized. It is likely difficult to join conversations or know how to manage yourself in typical social interactions.

One of the main reasons people have difficulty being assertive is because of social anxiety. We worry about what other people think of us and whether or not they will approve of us. This can make it very difficult to speak up for ourselves or to express our needs and wants.

One way to overcome this is to remind yourself that you are as worthy as anyone else and have just as much right to express yourself as anyone else does. It can also be helpful to remember that everyone is different and that not everyone will agree with you or approve of what you have to say. However, that doesn't mean that you shouldn't say it.

Practice Assertiveness

It helps to practice being assertive in small situations before working up to more difficult conversations. For example, you could start by expressing a dissenting opinion in a discussion with friends or family about something inconsequential. Once you feel more comfortable doing this, you could start speaking up in meetings at work or in other groups.

You can also practice assertiveness by role-playing with a friend or family member. This can be a helpful way to become more comfortable with expressing yourself and with learning how to manage difficult situations.

Remember, being assertive is a skill that can be learned. The more you practice, the better you will become at it. Just like with anything else, the key is to take it one step at a time.

Below are some suggestions for how you can practice being assertive:

In your everyday life:

- Try to express your opinions more often. This can be in conversation with friends, family, or colleagues.
- When you are in a group, try to contribute more often. This can be by sharing your ideas or offering your opinion on something. Don't be discouraged if at first your contributions aren't embraced. Continue to actively listen and stay involved.
- If you are in a meeting at work, try to speak up more. This can be by offering your ideas or asking questions.
- When you are out with friends or family, try to say what you want to do rather than going along with what everyone else wants to do.

In more challenging situations:

- If you are in a situation where you feel like you are being taken advantage of, try to say no.
- If you are in a situation where you feel like you are being treated unfairly, say so.
- If you are in a situation where you feel like someone is trying to control you, try to assert yourself. This can be difficult, but it is important to maintain your autonomy. Even a small resistance begins to send a message.

Remind Yourself That You Are Worthy

One of the main reasons people have difficulty being assertive is that they don't feel worthy or deserving of it.

They may feel like they are not good enough or don't deserve to speak up.

It is important to remind yourself that you deserve to take up space just as much as anyone else. You have just as much right to express yourself and be assertive as the rest of us.

Assert Yourself by Communicating Your Accomplishments

It can be difficult to communicate your accomplishments, as it may feel like bragging or being arrogant.

When you communicate your accomplishments, you are letting others know what you are capable of and that you value those skills and contributions. This can be a fantastic way to build relationships and trust with others who have similar interests. It can also help you to feel more confident in yourself.

If you are having trouble communicating your accomplishments, here are some tips:

- Start by writing down a list of your accomplishments. This can be anything, no matter how small you might think it is.
- Once you have your list, start sharing your accomplishments with others. You can do this in person, or you can share them online. For example, you can post them on social media or write about them in a blog post.
- When you share an accomplishment, explain why it is important to you or how you were able to pull it off. This will help others to understand why you are proud of them.

- Mention your accomplishment casually in a conversation about a related topic. Say you ran a 5k race last month when some colleagues are talking about their cross-fit class. Something like "where do you take that class? I've been looking for a new workout routine since I ran *x* race, maybe I'll check it out," is a simple way to build rapport and let people know a bit about you.
- Be proud of your accomplishments, and don't belittle them.

It is good practice to at least be mindful of the things you're capable of and the sacrifices you made to accomplish them.

Assert Yourself by Standing Up for Your Values

If you do not stand up for what you value, it will be difficult to find your people and tap into the best things life has to offer. Your values can be qualities like honesty and loyalty, or they can be interests like comics or baseball, or they can stem from cultural background or spiritual beliefs.

When you stand up for your values, you are telling others you will not tolerate anything less than what you deserve. This can be a great way to build relationships and trust with like-minded people. It can also help you feel more confident in yourself.

If you are having trouble standing up for what you believe in, here are some tips:

- Start by identifying what you value. Not everyone has a defined set of values and may not have a strong opinion on some important topics - that is fine. Once you identify values that are truly important to you, it will be easier to stand up for them.

- Become informed, discuss your point of view with others, and listen to opposing viewpoints so you can be confident in what you are saying.
- Be prepared to back up your beliefs with facts. This will make it easier to convince others that you are right.
- Your beliefs are no more important and no less important than the beliefs of others.
- Be respectful of other people's beliefs. Even if you do not agree with someone else's beliefs, you should still respect their right to have them.

Taking a stand for your values can be challenging, but it is vital. If you do not stand up for what you believe in, you will never get what you want in life. We must all understand that we live among billions of other people and the diversity of value systems is endless. To live together harmoniously, we must respect each other's values.

Key Takeaways

- Being assertive is key to successful communication.
- When you are assertive, you build better relationships, feel more confident, and get what you want in life without sacrificing your own happiness.
- You can start becoming assertive by sharing your accomplishments with others and standing up for what you believe in.

- There is a difference between being assertive and being aggressive.
- Start small and gradually work your way up the ladder of assertiveness.

Becoming assertive is a process that takes time and practice. Start small and gradually work your way up. Remember, being nice doesn't mean being a doormat. You have a right to your own opinions and beliefs, as long as they are fact-based and not hurtful to others. When you are assertive, you will build better relationships, feel more confident, and get what you want without sacrificing your happiness. Start asserting yourself!

Chapter 5
Make Small Talk Interesting

"That's all small talk is - a quick way to connect on a human level - which is why it is by no means as irrelevant as the people who are bad at it insist. In short, it's worth making an effort."

— Lynn Coady

Friendships begin with small talk and progress to long, in-depth discussions, and before you know it, you're concerned about the person. We frequently underestimate the power of small talk. While some dismiss it as meaningless, small talk establishes connections, jumpstarts conversations, builds relationships, and forms strong bonds.

Small talk is a polite and uncomplicated way to discuss unimportant topics. The ability to make small talk is regarded as a social skill and is a valuable tool for building rapport and finding common ground. It's an excellent way to break the ice and strike up a conversation with strangers.

In a world where technology and the internet have offered more means to connect and communicate with a lot of people, some still find it hard to have interesting conversations. There's either a moment of awkward silence, a recurrence of flat responses, or a discussion of boring and repetitive topics.

If you struggle with social anxiety to any extent or are an introvert, small talk can be difficult. It might even make you feel more anxious and undermine your confidence.

All of these factors combine to make many conversations threadbare, but after reading this chapter, this won't be the case because we'll be talking about how to make these little conversations interesting and productive.

Small Talk as a Social Lubricant

Small talk's intended purpose changes depending on the situation, but its primary objective is to facilitate social interaction in different adaptable ways. It's a good strategy and a bonding ritual for maintaining interpersonal distances despite its ostensibly less useful purpose than in-depth conversations.

It performs a variety of socially significant tasks, such as facilitating the establishment of bonds between coworkers, strangers, and friends. Because both parties can categorize and explore their social positions, it is especially helpful in relationships with new acquaintances.

At work, dates, family gatherings, and networking events, we're bound to start conversations with familiar faces and unfamiliar strangers. With less emphasis on why we engage in these types of conversations, few arguments for or assertions about the significance of small talk include:

1. Conversation Opener

A connection can be established between two speakers who do not know each other in a discussion. As a conversation starter, small talk allows two or more people who don't know each other to express positive and friendly intentions, laying the groundwork for communication.

It allows people to solidify each other's areas of expertise and reputation in business meetings or a formal setting. If both speakers already have a relationship, small talk can be used as a gentle introduction before moving on to more serious and functional topics. They can both signal their mood and perceive the mood of others through small talk.

In other informal settings, like at a bar, during a game, or on an outing, it is a great way to start group discussions and keep everyone engaged. What begins as a trivial discussion most of the time eventually evolves into a hearty conversation.

2. Ending Conversations

Small talk isn't for starting conversations only; it also helps you end them. It would be inappropriate to begin a conversation and then abruptly end it. Small talk helps to end conversations in a calm, friendly manner, leaving the person wanting to talk again.

3. Space Filler

The silence between two or more people can be quite awkward. It is uncomfortable and causes anxiety, but these gaps are better filled by using small talk as a tool.

A prolonged pause or break in communication is uncomfortable for people. Tension will increase as one talker might not want to interrupt or stop the other's speech. With small talk, tension is reduced, and a subject is opened up for discussion until an important subject is brought up.

4. Establish Trust

Whatever the subject, small talk serves as a sign that making friends and exchanging pleasantries is both possible and highly valued. Friendships do not develop through eye contact or head nodding; rather, the foundation is set by small talk.

Small talk plays a significant role in developing trust. It is improper to start a lengthy conversation without first building little rapport or trust. Even though it may seem insignificant, small talk is the foundation for greater relationships and deeper trust.

5. Warmth and Affection

Have you ever wanted to speak with, contact, or visit someone to share your thoughts or experiences with them? Whether on the phone or in person, you can also express your concerns for that person.

You don't need to be intense in your conversation—it could be a casual discussion about a doctor's appointment, about that surgery, a new baby, or a significant achievement at work or in academics—but that straightforward gesture demonstrates your concern.

Calling to see how their day went, what they have planned for the evening or weekend, or if you could come around sometime is small talk, but it demonstrates genuine interest and helps foster stronger and healthier relationships.

6. Create Opportunities

People frequently avoid pleasantries with office security guards, neighbors, or even making small talk with a coworker, but they forget that people are the foundation of our society.

The security guards you greet at the store, your neighbor or a total stranger you helped might be able to help you in your hour of need. You might brighten their day by acknowledging their presence and taking a minute out of your day to say hello. You might feel a larger sense of belonging to your community since you know more people in it.

They could give you advice on available jobs, the best places to shop, handymen, or even help you with repairs. Small talk comes off as chatty, but it has the potential to lead to opportunities you were unaware of.

Small talk plays a crucial role in fostering social interaction. Seemingly unimportant subjects can pave the way for lasting friendships and throw open doors to chances you never imagined. Even though they might not seem important at the moment, they might be in the future.

Social Awkwardness and How to Overcome It

Social anxiety has much more severe symptoms than shyness, including a persistent fear that interferes with relationships, work, school, and other activities. People who suffer from social anxiety are always concerned about social situations before, during, and after they occur.

Even though it's common for people to feel anxious before social gatherings, social anxiety sufferers find it particularly challenging. A persistent and crippling fear of social situations is referred to as social anxiety, also known as social phobia.

Children and teenagers are most likely to experience social anxiety, but it affects people of all ages. A study (Social Anxiety Centre) shows that social anxiety affects a whopping 15 million adults in the US and usually begins as early as age 7.

It is pretty common for people to get nervous at big events, when giving a presentation, or when doing something on a large scale, but when it starts to affect one's physical and mental state, it becomes a major issue.

People begin to worry about daily activities that require them to see strangers, go shopping, work, or go places and do things that require them to be seen or heard.

They find it difficult to do things in public because they worry that they are doing something embarrassing, like appearing incompetent or blushing, fear criticism, and making eye contact, all of which lead to low self-esteem.

Palpitations, trembling, profuse sweating, panic attacks caused by an overwhelming sense of fear, and eventually, depression or panic disorders are all byproducts of social anxiety.

Such conditions impede communication and socialization, resulting in a person who is a shadow of themselves, with low productivity and academic performance, negativity, isolation, poor social skills, and suicidal thoughts.

It is possible for symptoms of social anxiety to affect a person in particular settings but not in others. For instance, being exceedingly confident at work but shy around friends or acquaintances. If you're not used to public speaking but have been asked to give a wedding speech in front of hundreds of strangers, you may feel the heat.

When anxiety of any type rears its ugly head, it can be uncomfortable and even briefly debilitating. If you find yourself in an especially intense situation, it can be difficult to remain calm. A few coping strategies are:

1. Control Your Breathing

Anxiety causes your body to change in ways that are inconvenient for you. Your breathing rate changes, causing you to feel suffocated, dizzy, or tense. All of these changes make it difficult for you to maintain control of yourself during social situations.

The first step is to master your breathing. Several breath control techniques would be beneficial and help with other social anxiety symptoms. Get into a comfortable position, relax, and take slow, deep breaths.

2. Focus on Others

Anxiety has the effect of keeping you in your head. You can't pay attention to what's going on around you, and as thoughts, permutations, and different scenarios run through your head, you become terrified.

What you should do to help yourself is focus on the outside world rather than what's going on inside your head. This can be accomplished by actively listening to others. Listen to what they have to say rather than what that voice in your head is telling you. People can't tell how nervous you are; once you remember that, try to pay attention to others.

3. Use Your Senses

During a stressful situation, your senses of sight, smell, sound, taste, and touch help you relax. Chewing gum, smelling something pleasant, listening to music, or visualizing a calming image in your mind all help you relax. You should try whatever works for you. You might not try one that helps right away, so try a few different things and see which one sticks.

4. Get Out There

This might sound too difficult, but there is no other way to progress if you stay hidden within the confines of your home. Go out with your friends and try new things. It will be frightening, and it is important to recognize that you don't have to be as social as others, but you should try to go out occasionally.

You're not perfect, not everyone knows your best self, and their opinions don't matter; take risks because you never know what might happen.

5. Get Help When Necessary

Nervousness happens from time to time, but social anxiety does more than you can imagine. It has an impact on a person's social ability, which is a necessary skill in today's world. It's possible to overcome as one grows. Having a support system, taking charge of your health, and putting yourself out there will help you overcome it. If you believe you suffer from severe social anxiety, you should seek a professional evaluation.

Knowing When to Make an Exit

It can be difficult to maintain a conversation at times due to the attitude of the parties involved, the nature of the conversation, or the topic being discussed. At some point, there will be awkward silence during which people have nothing to discuss or contribute, causing the conversation to sour.

Usually, it isn't the speaker's fault, but if it continues for too long, the conversation dies and tension rises. An awkward moment of silence in a discussion does not indicate a lack of social skills; rather, it is the ideal time to exit that discussion or discuss another topic.

Nonetheless, here are a few pointers to avoid that awkward silence:

1. Accept the Silence

Recognize that not every silence is the result of an error on someone's part. In every discussion, there comes a time when a speaker runs out of words or topics to discuss, which explains the pause. Other times, the person is in pain and lacks the words to express how they feel.

Consider using nonverbal cues. Make eye contact, hug them, hold their hands, and observe the silence as a reflection of their emotional space.

The silence could be a natural pause or the result of someone making a thought-provoking statement that everyone feels the need to reflect on. The silence is awkward, but it could be for a good reason.

2. Start Another Conversation

If a topic is causing a lull in the conversation, take advantage of the time to come up with an alternative subject. Consider potential conversation topics before going to a social event. Think of a topic that the event attendees can relate to; you could talk about the event's theme and decorations or something unrelated that your audience would find interesting, like a national, sports, entertainment, or business topic.

If a conversation breaks down while you're with friends or in a small group setting, ask a question or try summarizing what they said; maybe they'll tell you more. You don't need any special abilities to start a conversation, ask questions, learn about the person, and get them to talk.

3. Ask Open Ended Questions

It's a conversation, not a monologue. Allow others to express themselves and ask questions to learn about their point of view. Don't ask simple ones that require a yes or no answer; instead, let them say what's on their mind and listen carefully to respond engagingly.

A conversation involves both talking and listening. When you speak, they listen, and when they speak, you listen. Talk to people with confidence and charisma. Smile more, make gestures with your hands to boost confidence, and listen to them while also finding a common topic to discuss. Listen carefully, keep an open mind, and sometimes accept silence as a graceful exit from the conversation.

Exercises to Make Small Talk Interesting

Little chatty conversations are majorly about trivial matters, but when you ramble on and on about assorted topics, the conversation shifts gears and becomes profound, laying the groundwork for a lasting friendship.

Some people believe they are experts at small talk; although there is no exact rule or school for getting good at it; simply doing a few things to get people talking and responding interactively will suffice.

Here are a few pointers to help you improve your small talk game:

1. Assume Good Things

One thing that stuck with us as we grew up was to avoid strangers. That worked for a while until you had to go out and talk to these people in person. Have you ever heard the expression "don't judge a book by its cover"? Apply the same rule when meeting new people. By assuming the best in people, start a conversation with them and give them the benefit of the doubt rather than the boring opening lines; 'can I know your name and what you do'-approach.

2. Use Your Environment

What you see and notice can serve as a friendly conversation starter. It is easier to strike up a conversation when you use cues from your surroundings. You can even start a conversation by asking, "How about this weather?" cliché as it may be. People proclaim to hate that question, yet they always engage.

3. Show Interest

Boredom ends a conversation more quickly than anything else. It results in awkward pauses and even stress. Instead of faking it, look for a subject both of you are interested in. Find a point of agreement, then build from there. It could be about anything. Use active listening and pose questions.

A conversation is a two-way activity in which both speakers must take part. There is no set formula for small talk but going into a conversation with an open mind, listening, and participating actively while talking about a shared interest are all excellent small talk techniques. Be confident, charming, and thoughtful to ensure that the conversation flows.

Key Takeaways

- Small talk is an informal discussion about unimportant and uncontroversial topics that are useful for starting conversations.
- Small talk serves as a conversation starter, filler, and means of establishing trust.
- Social anxiety impedes interpersonal communication, and it affects millions of teens and adults to some extent.
- Making deliberate efforts, such as attending social events, taking care of your health, and seeking help, when necessary, to overcome social anxiety.

- During conversations, awkward silences will occur. It could be due to a natural pause, intense emotions, or the topic of discussion.
- It's okay to accept awkward silence, use icebreakers, start a new conversation, or take the opportunity to exit the conversation.

When it comes to making small talk, there are no hard and fast rules; all you need to do is make an effort to listen, respond, and see the best in other people. Treat other people with kindness, show interest in what they're saying, and make sure the topics you bring up are engaging. Make an effort to maintain the flow of the conversation, encourage the other person to participate, and keep in mind that it is not all about you. Try shifting the focus to others by asking questions if you are uncomfortable speaking up at first.

The next chapter will introduce you to the potential and unique powers of written communication and how it can be an effective outlet for expression.

Chapter 6
Compelling Communication in the Digital Age

"Texting is a fundamentally sneaky form of communication, which we should despise, but it is such a boon we don't care. We are all sneaks now."

— Lynne Truss

In our fast-paced, constantly connected world, it's easy to forget the power of face-to-face communication. But as anyone who has ever had a heart-to-heart conversation knows, there's something special about being able to look someone in the eye and share your thoughts and feelings. When done well, writing can be an incredibly powerful way to connect with others. Most of us do not write eloquent texts or emails, however, and this rushed substitute for meaningful connection can be tricky.

Texting

It has become one of the most common forms of communication. While texts can be an efficient way to stay in touch with friends and family, this communication medium can easily lead to misunderstandings and conflict. To make sure your texts are sending the right message, it's important to consider both the content and the tone. The following are some guidelines for texting effectively:

- When it comes to the content of your text, be clear and concise. The recipient should be able to understand what you're trying to say without having to guess or interpret your words. Avoid using abbreviations or slang with someone less familiar to you.

- It's also important to be aware of the tone of your text. The tone can often be communicated more through the use of emojis and expressive language than through the actual words used. For example, if you want to come across as playful or friendly, you might use more emojis and exclamation points in your text. A well-placed emoji or funny GIF can inject some personality into your texts and add levity if you feel it's needed.

- Keep in mind that texts are often read out of context, so it's important to choose your words carefully. If you're not sure how the recipient will interpret what you've written, it's best to err on the side of caution. Be direct. If it sounds too direct or sterile, throw in a gif or emoji. Assume the recipient might misread what you've attempted to say, so be concise. With these guidelines in mind, texting can be a great way to stay connected.

Texting and Online Dating

When you're communicating via text, there are no facial expressions or body language to give you clues about what someone is thinking or feeling. When two people haven't met each other in person yet, there is no knowledge to inform assumptions, so we are essentially using our imagination when reading texts. That's why it's important to pay attention to the words you use and the tone of your messages. Be hyper-vigilant of potential miscommunication, and give the other person the benefit of the doubt.

Texting can help you get a better sense of someone's personality and how they communicate. It can also be a fun way to flirt, build rapport and keep the conversation flowing. Using positive, upbeat language will help create a strong connection with your match. If you ever need a little help getting the conversation started, try asking open-ended questions that will encourage your match to share more about themselves.

While face-to-face communication is ideal, it's not always possible. This method of communication is based on the idea that we can use words to create powerful emotional reactions in others. In other words, we can influence how someone feels about us by carefully choosing our words.

Use these three strategies to make your texts more compelling:

1. **Send positive messages:** Be sure to send messages that are positive and upbeat. Avoid negativity, as it will only

turn the other person off. If you have a sarcastic sense of humor, save it for when you meet in person. Sarcasm does not translate well to text, especially when you don´t know each other yet.

2. **Use strong words:** Choose your words carefully and use language that is strong and emotive. Words have a lot of power, so use them wisely! Think twice before texting something that could have a double meaning – be very clear with your words.

3. **Use active language:** Avoid passive language or phrases like "I think" or "maybe we could." Go for active phrases like "I'd love to see that exhibit, would you like to join?" or "Why don't we try that new restaurant?". Speaking like this conveys interest and decisiveness.

Texting and Romantic Relationships

Couples today are nearly as likely to communicate through a screen as they are to communicate face-to-face. While texting can be a convenient way to stay in touch, it can also create new challenges.

Couples may find themselves arguing about things via text, or using text to continue a tense conversation that began in person. Since texts can be easily misconstrued, they have the potential to create explosive misunderstandings. Couples may also find that texting reduces their ability to communicate effectively. When trying to communicate complex emotions or topics through text, it can be easy for messages to get lost in translation. Continuing a fight that started face-to-face via text is a recipe for disaster and should be avoided.

There are countless emotional aspects to conflict resolution that simply cannot be conveyed through a text message. If you are prone to exchanging heated texts with anyone in your life, think about how many fights you've resolved over text. Any? Or does texting about it merely prolong the conversation until an impasse is reached and the matter is resolved in a later conversation?

Despite the challenges texting can pose for romantic relationships, there are also some benefits. Texting is great for staying in touch with your partner throughout the day. It can also be a convenient way to communicate when you are unable to talk on the phone or meet in person. In addition, when used appropriately, texting can build intimacy and connection in a relationship.

There are, of course, some exceptions to the rule. Some people find it more comfortable to communicate through text, as this method gives them time to think about what they want to say without being interrupted. This can allow for more thoughtful and meaningful conversations. Ultimately, whether texting is positive or negative for romantic relationships depends on how it is used. When used thoughtfully and with consideration of your partner's needs, texting can be a great tool for building intimacy and connection.

Writing Good Emails

A friend of mine once told me she just needed to respond to a few emails and then she'd be ready to leave her office. We finally met up two hours later. Work Email has become a monster that prevents people from doing their real job.

It's difficult to juggle all the communication we're expected to participate in while staying above water. Crafting a good email should be quick and get you results.

Tips for Written Communication at Work

If you're looking for ways to stand out and get a response, the words you craft must be compelling and attention-grabbing. Here are some examples of how you can do that:

1. Use strong language that shows you take the message seriously and value your colleague's time.

2. Keep it brief. Avoid fluff and unnecessary pleasantries.

3. Give a deadline (or ask). Make it clear when you need a response.

4. Use collaborative language. People enjoy collaborating, they ignore demands.

5. Avoid passive language. Be direct about what is needed and if you have an idea of how to achieve it.

6. Follow up! If you don't hear back within a reasonable timeframe, reach out again to make sure they received and understood your message.

7. If you get stuck writing, consider a phone call instead. It could take a fraction of the time and get you way more information.

Tips That Guarantee a Response to Your Emails

You know the feeling all too well. You spend way too much time crafting the perfect email, hit "send," and then...crickets. When you're emailing someone you don't know well or even someone you do know but want to establish a rapport with, it's important to make a good impression. Whether you're trying to network, grow your business, or simply make a new friend, here are some tips for writing emails that will guarantee a response.

1. **Pay attention to the subject line.** Keep it concise and clear so that the recipient knows what the email is about at a glance. Berating them with a long, rambling subject line is not going to encourage them to read your message. Posing a question as the subject line is a great sales tactic that could make sense in certain other situations. A question will grab attention.

2. **Be authentic and friendly.** People can tell when you're being genuine, so don't try to sound like someone you're not.

3. **Make sure you're not coming across as overly formal or stiff.** No one likes being on the receiving end of an email that feels like a robot could have written it.

4. **Ask questions.** This shows that you're interested in learning more about the person you're emailing. It also allows them to respond and start a conversation.

5. **Offer value.** What can you offer that will benefit the other person? Whether it's an article you think they would enjoy, an introduction to someone they should meet, or just a helpful tip, make sure there's something in it for them.

6. **Say thank you.** Always end your email with a thank you.

By following these simple tips, you can get the response you're looking for and save yourself the headache of wondering why your emails are being ignored.

Key Takeaways

- Text is a great way to stay in touch but a difficult way to fully express emotions.
- As our world becomes saturated in a text conversation, try to remain personable and concise.

Perhaps you've been texting or emailing someone you have yet to meet. Whether it's a client, a date, or a new buddy, first impressions are important. The chapter will make sure that you put your best foot forward when meeting someone new.

Chapter 7
Make a Great First Impression

"First impressions matter - experts say we size up new people in somewhere between 30 seconds and two minutes"

— Elliott Abrams

First impressions are the initial conclusions we draw when we connect with a new person. These conclusions are formed based on the person's mannerisms, how they speak, the way they are dressed, and myriad factors ranging from vague and superficial to profound and intuitive.

To understand someone to a reasonable extent, you need to spend ample time with them. No reasonable person will judge someone entirely based on a first impression, but there are moments in life when it is critical to wow your audience quickly. First impressions do not wait or ask why before drawing conclusions. Without realizing all the mechanics at work when we form a first impression of somebody, our mind paints a detailed picture of what we should expect from them.

As you read through this chapter, remember that making a great first impression is all about you expressing your authentic self. First impressions tend to be based in large part on a host of superficial qualities. When we are comfortable and feel like we belong, we tend to effortlessly give off a good first impression.

No one expects to gain insights into your soul on the first meeting, so the goal is to display authenticity. This can come in the form of politeness, interest, and confidence. People are very good at picking out inauthentic behavior and the only sure way to spoil your first impression is to present a false image of yourself. A first impression is not a chance to advertise yourself; it's simply a chance to allow people to warm up to you, and vice versa.

Making a Good First Impression at an Interview

People form opinions about you in a matter of seconds. In an interview, you must shake off your nerves and allow your authentic personality to shine. A shocking number of corporate HR managers and small business owners will admit to valuing culture fit more than professional experience when hiring new talent. Most job postings receive hundreds if not thousands of applicants, so being likable in an interview goes a long way. If the interviewer believes you will be easy to work with, you have an excellent chance of landing the job over someone more qualified than you. If they had a pleasant conversation and believe you are willing to do what it takes to develop the skills required by the role, they are more likely to move you further along in the hiring process.

No matter how tense you are, try to find a way to relax without seeming flippant. If you're being interviewed by your potential future boss, they are likely not an expert at interviewing people; they are an expert in their field. Unless you're being interviewed by someone like Oprah, assume the person interviewing you may be slightly unsure of their skills in this realm. They may only interview a few people per year and are likely to ask canned questions because there is simply no science to this. Most people conducting interviews are somewhat uncomfortable to be doing so. Be authentic and show your true colors while trying to learn all you can about your interviewer.

Follow these tips to ace your next interview:

1. Concentrate on the Interviewer

Focus on the interviewer because they are the most important person at that moment. You must give them your undivided attention. Do not sell yourself too quickly by talking more than listening. Be genuine about your desire to get the job.

You can directly ask the interviewer what they need most out of the job description. Listen to all of their needs. To demonstrate that you have been paying attention, ask questions that are specific to each need to obtain additional information. Getting them to talk about their company will make them more comfortable with you. This is a fantastic opportunity to learn more about the position you're applying for. Always keep an eye out for potential red flags, as these can be great questions for you to ask later.

Now that you know their needs, share the skills, experience, and personality traits you possess that fit what they are looking for. Be tactful when discussing areas that lack experience. You don't need to come right out and profess your deficits, but be sure to express confidence that you'll be able to learn any skills you're not entirely comfortable with already. It's all about authenticity. Maintain positive body language, make eye contact, and smile when appropriate. Maintain eye contact during the interview, whether online or in person. This shows that you're confident and you're paying attention to what they're saying.

2. Keep Your Composure

Maintain good posture and demonstrate your interest in each of the interviewers. Try not to become disoriented, distracted, or camera shy. I like the saying *never let them see you sweat.* Stay focused.

You can take solace in the fact that the interviewer is just as concerned as you are about choosing the right person for the job. If you have an in-person interview, sit up straight and avoid slouching, pull your shoulders back, and keep your cool throughout the process. If you notice yourself fidgeting, reign it in but don't overthink it. Showing uncomfortable body language will not ruin your shot at the job, but obsessing over anything negative you observe about yourself can sabotage an otherwise great interview. Remember, the only reason you could have been invited to the interview is that you are very likely the best person for the job.

When attending an interview via video call, make sure the sound, lighting, and video quality are all excellent. The background should be clean and organized to reflect your personality. Turn on the camera before logging in to make sure you're not backlit and nothing is distracting in the field of view. Make sure everyone around you knows what's going on to minimize the chance of distraction. If you happen to get interrupted during the interview, this is an excellent opportunity to show your interviewer how you react when things don't go according to plan. Keep your cool, stay focused, and remain pleasant.

3. Ask Questions

You should go into the interview with a few questions prepared from the research you've done on the company and the role.

Your first question can be directed at the interviewer to build rapport. You might ask them why they chose to work for that company and what they like best about its culture. Find out what they enjoy about their job. See if they have any advice they would give to someone in your position just starting at the company.

4. Reflect Your Interviewer's Behavior

Matching your interviewer's communication style can help things along. People speak in various ways; some speak abruptly and quickly, while others talk slowly. Take note of the interviewer's cadence and reflect it back to them.

If your interviewer speaks slowly and clearly, you should do the same. This will give them the impression that they have found someone similar to them, and they will feel more at ease and comfortable. Mirroring speech patterns is a subtle way of indicating agreement and willingness to compro-mise. You might consider using their name once or twice during the interview. When someone's name is mentioned in a conversation, they tend to respond with interest. It captures their attention and fosters a sense of intimacy. Mentioning their name is effective, but don't overdo it.

Mirroring, also called isopraxism, is imitation. We copy each other as a way to comfort one another—and you can see this behavior in humans (as well as some animals). People can form bonds and establish trust by matching their speech patterns, body language, vocabulary, and tone—all unconscious processes. You're rarely aware that you're doing it until someone points out the uncanny resemblance between your posture while speaking with a new acquaintance and those you adopt when talking to an old friend at a party.

A fundamental biological principle—fear of the unknown, attraction to familiarity—accounts for our fascination with this phenomenon. The same concept applies to our attraction to similar people and ideas. This makes us feel safe—we know what we're dealing with when we encounter someone who shares our values.

Be Positive and Realistic

Being positive, authentic, and in touch with reality will make you stand out in any situation. Do not be derogatory or negative about your former workplace or anything at all during the interview.

It may sound contradictory but be open about things you didn't like about a previous job or wouldn't like about this one. Speak about these matters in a neutral way and allow your interviewers to see your fundamental values. If you like to work independently and can't stand being micromanaged, this is worth mentioning in an interview. Your interviewers will appreciate your candor and will likely be encouraged to share meaningful information about the role that will help you decide whether it is the right fit for you.

Making a Great First Impression When Meeting Your In-Laws

It can be intimidating to meet your partner's family. Meeting your future in-laws for the first time can leave you feeling overwhelmed with the desire to impress them. They will not form their full opinion of you based on the first impression, but how you present yourself during your first meeting is important.

What your potential in-laws feel or think about you after meeting you for the first time will play a significant role in determining the nature of your relationship with them in the long run.

To start off on the right foot, make sure you:

1. Dress Properly

It may sound old school, but the way we dress is absolutely a form of communication. Putting a bit of extra effort into our appearance for certain occasions represents to others that we respect that occasion and the people around us. Wear something that allows you to relax and enjoy yourself. Put on something comfortable that makes you feel confident.

2. Bring a Gift

Bring a gift. Everyone enjoys receiving gifts, and giving one to your in-laws will help make a good impression. It doesn't have to be anything expensive. You can bring wine, cookies, or cake. Find out what your partner's family likes to avoid giving them something they won't appreciate.

3. Compliment Them

Sincere compliments can win people over. Look around their home and compliment the decor, table setting, family pictures, or furniture. Don't overdo it by complimenting everything you see; it can seem fake if you do it too much.

4. Speak Clearly

Avoid being obnoxious or loud when meeting your in-laws for the first time. Don't yell or use vulgar language. Pay attention to what you say and do.

5. Be on Your Best Behavior

Overdo it with your manners. You can't be too polite, as long as it's genuine. Your in-laws are interested in how you treat their child, and simple gestures such as saying "please," or offering to help out with something small can mean a lot.

6. Focus on Them

This family may soon become yours, so try to get to know them. Don't cling to your phone or partner. This isn't the time or place for public displays of affection (PDA), so resist the urge to kiss and hug your partner whenever possible. For the time being, concentrate on the family and your autonomy.

Feel free to speak with various family members, both old and young. You can have some fun with the kids. If cousins, uncles, and aunts are present, learn about them. This can be interpreted as your willingness to establish relationships with the extended family.

7. Show You Are Willing to Help

Ask where you can be of assistance if you see an opportunity. This isn't about proving your worth or falling into a submissive dynamic off the bat, but rather the goal is to communicate that you can participate as part of the family unit.

8. Compliment Your Partner

The family will undoubtedly enjoy hearing about the nice attributes that attract you to your partner. Praise your partner in front of your in-laws.

9. Thank Them

When it's time to leave, thank them for their hospitality. It's critical that they know you had an enjoyable time.

10. Be Polite to Everyone in the Family

They may ignore you or give you an attitude that makes your visit uncomfortable if you are rude. Don't walk in as if you own the place; know your limits and act accordingly.

11. Avoid Sensitive Issues

Bringing up topics like politics, money, sex, and religion is a tricky thing in most conversations, and this is no exception. If you are asked for your opinion on a touchy subject, feel free to give it. If tensions arise, remember the art of active listening. Be authentic, be inquisitive, and respect everyone's differences.

Your goal during the first visit is to make a good impression. Instead of sugarcoating your personality in an attempt to impress, be yourself and let them like you for who you are. Have fun, and in time, everything else will fall into place.

How to Make a Great First Impression When Meeting a New Potential Client

It is impossible to overstate the importance of making a good first impression when meeting with potential clients. It only takes a few seconds to form an opinion about someone.

A first impression can determine if a client becomes a customer. As an executive in your company, demonstrate your company's dependability and quality through everything you do during the meeting.

The following suggestions will help you impress your next client:

1. Do Background Research

Conduct preliminary research on the potential client. Prior to the meeting, you should be familiar with your client's target market, company size, values, specializations, and challenges.

One of the easiest places to find this information might be on the client's social media handles if applicable. Examine their posts to learn about their company culture and values. Check out individuals' LinkedIn profiles to obtain important information that will assist you in making personal connections with the client.

2. Arrive on Time

This shows that you are concerned about the meeting. It also implies that your company will prioritize customers during business transactions. Arriving late demonstrates irresponsibility and disregard for the client. Punctuality communicates respect and reliability.

3. Enter with Confidence

Exude confidence and be polite to everyone. Pay attention to your body language and the nonverbal cues you are giving off. Speak clearly and avoid rapid banter.

4. Take Advantage of Small Talk

Small talk helps build social relationships, so find common ground with the client to ease tension before the meeting. Making connections like this will show that you are friendly and genuine, not a robot who is there only to talk business.

If you are aware of common interests, bring those up. Don't go overboard with small talk; build rapport and move on.

5. Connect to their Needs

Ask questions that demonstrate your interest in your client's company. Your questions should indicate that you are actively participating in the conversation. This does not imply that you should ask irrelevant questions or make the client repeat themselves. Ask targeted questions based on information they have already given you, or that you have learned during your preparations.

6. Reinforce the Conversation with Non-Verbal Cues

Display coordinated, cheerful, and confident body language. Consider the message your posture conveys. You should speak softly. Keep your arms open and lean forward to demonstrate that you are welcoming.

As the client speaks, nod to show your agreement at regular intervals. Avoid crossing your arms, slouching, checking the time, or looking around the room when you should be listening.

7. Loosen Up

Your client should feel at ease and comfortable when doing business with you. Make a joke or tell a story to relieve tension and create a positive impression.

8. Follow Up

Your follow-up should summarize what you discussed and add value. If you did not set the next meeting already, do so here or determine the next steps. Express gratitude for their time.

How to Remain Calm before Making a First Impression

A first impression only takes seconds to be formed, and sometimes it is critical to make the most of this first contact with someone new. The focus should never be on impressing your audience, but rather on communicating authentically and allowing your personality to shine through any potential awkwardness.

You can help yourself achieve this goal by doing the following:

- Be on time to avoid tension.
- Be yourself because pretending to be someone else will keep you on edge.

- Smiling is contagious, so put it on even before you meet the expected person.
- Have confidence in yourself and know you are unique.
- Use small talk to relieve tension and remain relaxed.
- Maintain a positive attitude and mindset. Pay close attention to every detail because failing to do so will cause you to become disorganized.

Key Takeaways

Making a Good First Impression for an Interview

- Focus on the interviewer.
- Maintain your composure.
- Be positive, authentic, and genuine.

Making a Great First Impression When Meeting Your In-Laws

- Be yourself.
- Dress appropriately.
- Be on your best behavior.
- Compliment them.
- Avoid overindulging in alcohol.
- Be outspoken and expressive.

Making a Great First Impression When Meeting a New Potential Client

- Conduct preliminary research on the potential client.
- Be on time.
- Ask questions that demonstrate your interest in your client's company.
- Bring a notepad with you.

You only get one shot at a first impression, so position yourself to make the most of it. Be genuine, confident, and relaxed. Staying calm will help you make a great impression. Be authentic because people have a great ability to detect false behavior.

Chapter 8
Public Speaking

"By failing to prepare, you are preparing to fail."

— Benjamin Franklin

Preparation is essential for delivering your message with confidence. This involves researching both your message and the target audience, as well as practicing beforehand. You'll find that all the steps you should take before delivering your message are covered in this chapter.

Understand Your Message

What message are you attempting to convey? This should be the first question you answer. Your response will help you evaluate the content of your message. Is the message stand-alone or a component of a larger one? If you've already made notes, now is a good time to review them to make sure they are clear. At this point in the planning process, it is more important to concentrate on comprehending your message than on its delivery or reception by your audience.

Conduct Proper Research

Your audience is counting on you to speak authoritatively about whatever message you have for them. This is why you should conduct a lot of in-depth research on the subject matter. Study as many useful resources as you can, jot down as many questions you have about the subject, and then look for the answers to those questions in more resources. Learn the lingo and be prepared to answer questions. This phase may feel like a never-ending cycle, but it will pay off in the end when your message is delivered and your audience sees you as an authority in the field.

Get Comfortable with Your Voice

I am not a natural when it comes to public speaking, it is a skill I learned over time. I had to overcome my fear of speaking to a crowd early in my career and the experience nearly paralyzed me.

The best piece of advice someone gave me back then was to read out loud to myself in the weeks before my presentation. I spent a few minutes every morning reading loudly to myself from blogs, Reddit threads, the news, anything I was reading at the time. Taking it a step further, you can record yourself while you do this and then watch or listen back. The point of the exercise is to get over the massive discomfort of hearing your own voice speaking words that you did not think up. It is common for this to make people feel insecure and overly critical, and I hope you don't fall into that trap. Observe the way you speak, pick out some things you'd like to change, and keep practicing.

Put the Message into Sections

After you have fully comprehended your message, you should determine the most effective way to break it down into subtopics, bullet points, or sections - anything to make it easier to digest. This is also a good time to make a note of any words or phrases you want to stand out in your message; these are the words you should emphasize. Check for any potential questions your audience may have. If you take your time with this, you will come up with a list of possible questions from your audience, part of which will be verbal, while others will be rhetorical. Organizing your message into sections allows you to stay organized during delivery, maintain your flow, and ensure your audience is never left behind.

Develop the Message

Once you clearly understand your message and have broken it down into sections, take your time to develop it. Focus on one section at a time, making sure each one contributes to conveying the overall message and is cohesive. This evolution will also include the removal of elements you believe to be irrelevant (even if true) to the goal of your message. This is where you schedule the amount of time you will devote to each section of the message and the stories and examples you will use in illustrating each point. Investing enough time in crafting your message from both your own and the audience's points of view is important. To achieve this, think about organizing your message under the following subheadings:

Title: Use this to capture the attention of your audience and pique their interest.

Introduction: This allows you to prepare your audience for what is to come. A brief sneak peek sets expectations and helps the audience to stay focused.

Body: This is where you give all the explanations, illustrations, and examples. Keep sections short and concise.

Conclusion: This section allows you to review what you've done so far. In a few sentences, summarize everything you have presented. Summarize any questions you received as well, if possible and appropriate.

After you've planned your message and its flow, you should prepare yourself with your audience in mind. Let's take a look at how you do it together.

Study Your Audience

Understanding your audience is critical for conveying your message and ensuring its reception. You can send the same message to different types of people and have them react differently. Conveying the same message to a group of professionals will differ from conveying it to a group of students, farmers, or residents of mixed professions. Knowing your audience necessitates researching them before delivering your message. What information do you have about them and their behavioral patterns? How long can you keep them focused on your message? What audiovisual aids could help you get your message across more effectively?

Find out about others who have had success with your target audience and study what made them successful. This will enable you to approach them with equal or even greater success. This brings us to the point where you create an audience persona. When you've gathered enough information about your target audience, make a persona out of it to see how well your message matches what you've created.

Build Rapport with Your Audience

If you don't build trust with your audience, even if you have a great message, it will not come across well in your delivery. For your audience to unwind and pay attention to your message, you must establish a connection with them and earn their trust. So how do you build this relationship?

1. Confident Body Language

Your mode of transmission is extremely important. Add a smile to each greeting or exchange of pleasantries, handshake, or as you approach the podium. A smile on your face reassures and relaxes your audience. It conveys warmth and excitement. Instead of making the stage look like a hideout for you, show confidence by getting close to your audience. If you have a table or a lectern between you and them, go above and beyond to reach out to them. This helps to create the necessary connection between you and them.

2. Stay Relaxed

This may be your first time speaking in front of an audience this size. Even if you feel anxious, maintain a calm demeanor. Your nerves aren't showing nearly as much as you think they are. Take your time, take breaks as needed, and then continue. This is better than making sounds that give your audience the impression you are unsure of what you're saying. As their confidence in you and what you have to say increases, they loosen up and pay closer attention to you. Focus on your breath - shallow breaths make it difficult to speak while deep breaths are proven to have a calming effect. If your voice wavers at first, power through it and allow it to gain strength as you continue.

3. Focus on Your Audience

The focus of your presentation should be on your audience, not on yourself. Sometimes it helps to use relatable personal anecdotes to help them connect your message to their own personal experiences. Reach out to them, discuss issues they have raised verbally or in writing, discuss your findings of potential issues they may be dealing with, and go over some potential solutions. This shows your audience that you understand them and have what they need, which aids in the development of rapport.

4. Keep It Interactive

Always find a way to elicit a reaction or engagement from your audience. Don't keep talking without pausing to gauge their reactions and responses. When you ask questions and receive genuine responses, you will have a much bigger impact on your audience. Also, allowing them to ask you questions and taking your time to respond will increase their trust in you.

5. Embrace Dissenting Opinions

Expect opposing viewpoints if your presentation is interactive and receive them gracefully. By inviting different opinions, you will show your expertise and demonstrate your respect for the audience. Responding to critiques or opposition gives you a chance to deliver a more profound message.

Non-Verbal Cues

Another aspect to consider when preparing to deliver your message is nonverbal communication. It includes everything you do about your presentation other than what you say. Your message is what you say to the people, and how you say it is determined by your gesture, attitude, and carriage. Your audience, on the other hand, sends nonverbal messages through their attitudes while you speak to them. We will look at nonverbal communication from both the speaker's and the audience's perspectives.

As a speaker, you must prepare for more than merely delivering a message. You will make a few changes to yourself which will help give meaning to your words as you speak. Let us take a look at a few of them:

1. Keep Your Head Up

Holding your head high exudes self-assurance and demonstrates that you are proud of both who you are and what you are accomplishing at this moment. The more assuredly you move around the stage, the more control you'll have over the environment.

2. Keep Eye Contact

Maintaining constant eye contact with your audience boosts your confidence and strengthens the connection you have with them. This should be done with a smile on your face while still sharing your message. This ought to be enough to divert your attention away from yourself and toward the people listening to you.

3. Make Gestures with Your Hands

Do not be rigid or cling to the lectern in front of you. As you speak, move away from it and use hand gestures. The more natural your hand gestures appear, the more unique and self-assured you appear in front of your audience. Make certain you are not faking it, as your audience will notice if your gestures are robotic.

4. Express Yourself with Your Face

As you speak, make facial expressions correspond to your words. For example, displaying anger on your face communicates additional understanding to your audience when discussing an angry moment or situation. When you have success stories to share, show them off with your excitement. When discussing a sad situation, put on a glum expression for a few moments before proceeding. This way, your audience will connect with your words through your expressions.

5. Make Good Use of Your Stage

Moving around, even a little bit, helps you maintain control while delivering your message. Make sure your movement is in sync with your hand gesture and the flow of your message.

6. Pause from Time to Time

This gives you a chance to relax, take a breath, and then go on. Additionally, it gives your audience a chance to process all of the information you have been dumping on them.

As you perform the aforementioned actions, pay attention to your audience to detect any nonverbal cues they might be giving you. You can better read your audience by being aware of these cues.

7. Check the Energy Level

After a long speech, your audience begins to show signs of tiredness and lack of interest. Perhaps you've been talking for too long, and they're getting bored. It is critical for you to recognize these signs and know how to best reignite their energy, call a break, or end the presentation for the day. Other tricks you could use to re-energize your audience include:

· Telling an exciting story. It could be a personal story or something that happened around you. Anything to pique their interest again before you proceed

· Asking a question and insisting on their participation by suggesting answers. This reconnects them with you and can reawaken their interest.

· Telling a joke, perhaps about a popular event, and giving everyone a chance to laugh before proceeding.

8. Check Individual Reactions

If you notice that someone in your audience isn't paying attention, ask them to make a contribution or if they have a question.

9. Know When to Get Informal

You will need to pause the entire presentation at times to be more informal with your audience, allowing them to relax from the formal and uptight atmosphere in the room. Make everyone do something, such as stand, move around, or say hello to someone next to them. These things cause them to relieve themselves briefly before you proceed.

Importance of Preparing Your Message

In many ways, preparing your message keeps you on top of your game. Let's take a look at the advantages of planning your message:

- Planning ahead of time allows you to master the message.
- It allows you to get a taste of what your presentation will be like.
- It allows you to learn about your audience before meeting them.
- It also assists you in learning your stage before getting on it. These details may appear insignificant, but they are crucial to a speaker.
- Planning your message will help you stay organized throughout. Even if you have to take a detour, you know where to return to.
- Seeing how you prepared ahead of time, you can deliver your message completely without missing any parts.
- You are well-prepared for possible audience questions, dissenting opinions, and other surprises. Preparation arms you against unforeseen events.
- Knowing you are prepared gives you confidence as you deliver your presentation.
- Your audience deserves the best, and you will please them by planning your message ahead of time.

- You would gain your audience's trust and recommendation.

Key Takeaways

- Have a clear message
- Know your audience
- Avoid repetition in your presentation
- Know when to take a pause
- Maintain a positive attitude
- Pay attention to your audience's nonverbal cues.

Preparation is critical for success, and this determines the proper delivery of your message. Strive to always keep your audience's attention. Winning your audience's trust is essential to making your presentation more engaging and interesting.

In the next chapter, we will be exposing you to the art of negotiation. Keep on reading to improve your negotiation skills.

Chapter 9
Learning the Art of Negotiation

"The art of negotiation is perhaps what most deeply distinguishes man from the animals, and it is this art, and this will to negotiate that has brought man forward and elevated him beyond the animals."

— Harry Martinson

We tend to think of negotiation as a business term, but you are involved in small-stakes negotiations on a nearly daily basis. Despite its harsh or rigid connotations, a negotiation is a simple act of communication that can be as innocuous as deciding where to meet a friend for lunch. You two will determine a location that is mutually convenient, has good food and suits both of your budgets. You probably wouldn't think of such a simple interaction as a negotiation, but the same factors that go into making this tiny decision can also be applied to negotiating a raise, closing a deal, or smoothing over an ongoing conflict with someone close to you.

Negotiation is both an art and a science. It is an art because it involves perceptions, emotions, and tactics that can be employed to achieve mutually agreeable outcomes. Negotiation is a science because there are some fundamental rules you can use to achieve desired results. Many people believe in a "win-lose" approach to negotiations, however, a good deal is always mutually beneficial.

The goal of negotiation is to reach an agreement that will last over time and is never about strong-arming someone into agreeing to something that doesn't work for them. To be sustainable, this agreement must incorporate elements that satisfy the interests and concerns of both parties. It is an opportunity to reach a mutually beneficial agreement. Negotiation is about making choices—choices about what you want and why you want it; choices about how you communicate with other people to get what you want from them; and choices about when and where to negotiate. You may have guessed it at this point, but to be a great negotiator, you must be a great listener. Active listening and assertiveness come together as critical negotiation skills.

The better you understand your counterpart, the better you'll be at negotiating with them. The more you understand negotiation, the better equipped you will be to assert your wants and needs collaboratively. This chapter will help you understand the process of negotiation and teach you to be a respectful, assertive negotiator without having to do much more than ask great questions.

Life Is a Negotiation

In a negotiation, there are two essential goals: to gather information and to influence behavior. The first part, gathering information, is frequently neglected and this is where most negotiators fail. It is impossible to influence behavior, persuade someone to see your point of view or sell a product or service if you do not first determine what is motivating your counterpart's behavior and decision-making process.

Every aspect of your life depends on how well you negotiate. As a child, you learned to negotiate when you asked for permission to do something that required your parents' approval. If you wanted to go somewhere, play with certain friends or use certain toys, you had to ask for them. How many times have we heard a parent make a counteroffer to a child who asked for a later bedtime? As an adult, negotiation takes on a more serious meaning. It often occurs behind closed doors, and the stakes are much higher. Negotiation skills you learned early in life tend to become part of your communication style as an adult. The following are some examples of how negotiation can affect your life:

- You may negotiate with your boss for a raise or a promotion.
- You may negotiate with a partner about who does what chores around the house.
- You may negotiate with your spouse about where to spend your vacation.
- You may negotiate with a friend about where to meet for lunch.
- You may negotiate with a car dealer to get the best price for the latest model.

Before the Negotiation

You should always enter a negotiation prepared, no matter the stakes. What exactly it is that you want? Why is it important to you? How does it benefit the other party? What leverage do you have? Are there alternatives if the other party refuses to partake? After all, negotiations take place when both sides have something to gain or lose from the outcome of their discussions.

Getting to Yes, written by Fisher, Ury, and Patton in 1981, outlines the four main elements of principled negotiation. Consider these elements while preparing to negotiate to ensure it takes place fairly and rationally.

1. Separate the People from the Problem

This principle is often overlooked in negotiations but can be one of the most important aspects. When people feel personally attacked or put down, they become defensive and less likely to agree with what you have to say. By separating the person from the problem, you help them focus on finding solutions instead of getting caught up in emotions. The key to this is to stay away from personal attacks and stick to the facts. For example, if you want a raise but your boss isn't willing to give you one, don't say something like, "I feel as though I am not fairly compensated for my work here. What do you think about giving me a raise?" Instead, focus on the leverage you have by the role you perform. Mention how that role contributes to the company and how it is compensated in the wider job market. If your experience and tenure are not easily replaced, your boss will want to negotiate with you. Never look at getting a raise as a negotiation between your boss and you; your boss is not the problem; the salary is the focus. A more effective strategy is a collaborative approach that gets your boss thinking of you as a teammate rather than a sparring partner, someone he or she would like to help.

The key to making this work is to be calm and rational. If you become emotional, it will be hard for your boss to listen to what you are saying. If you place the blame on your boss for giving you a low salary, the response will be defensive. The more facts you can provide, the more likely your counterpart will listen to what you have to say.

2. Focus on Interests, Not Positions

Negotiators often waste time trying to find a compromise between two extreme positions. In principled negotiation, negotiators go beyond positional bargaining to find common interests. The goal is to build on each person's interests and come up with options that satisfy those interests. The best way to do this is to ask questions and listen carefully to the answers. You want to find out what each person wants, why they want it, what they are willing to give up getting it, and how their interests can be met without compromising yours.

Imagine that two siblings disagree about whether to host their parents' anniversary party at a restaurant or in the family home. They could accuse each other of being selfish or unreasonable and turn this into a heated argument. A better outcome is produced when each considers what is at the core of their siblings' decision-making process. One doesn't have any time to devote to preparation due to a demanding job, while the other is not in the financial position to cover the costs associated with renting out a venue. By gathering that information, the understanding that neither is arguing for the sake of getting their way allows for effective negotiating by targeting the pain point rather than the position or point of view. They research restaurants that would be suitable for the party and decide to host it at a relatively inexpensive spot. One sibling pays a bit more and the other acts as the organizer, dedicating more time. Inter-est-based bargaining can create solutions that address the needs of all parties involved.

3. Invent Options for Mutual Gain

Often, negotiators settle for an agreement that is satisfactory to both sides only after trying out several alternatives and failing to reach other agreements. In principled negotiation, negotiators spend more time brainstorming and evaluating options than they initially planned before deciding on an agreement. In negotiation, options refer to any possible way of satisfying a party's interests—from making deals and concessions to coming up with Plan B in case the first one doesn't work.

For instance, if one party wants to buy a house for $300,000 and the other is asking for $400,000, both sides can consider possible options to come up with a mutually agree-able price. A principled negotiator would not just settle on the first offer made by the seller but would be open to exploring other options, such as offering $375,000 or even $350,000.

Price is never the singular driving factor of any negotiation, so be sure to explore other terms, options, or perks that can be negotiated in addition to the money involved.

4. Insist on Using Objective Criteria

To come up with objective criteria, negotiators should clearly define the problem and its possible solutions. Once they have done so, they can then create a list of possible options based on their needs and interests as well as those of their counterparts. The more accurate and complete this list is, the easier it will be for everyone to find common ground.

Once this list is complete, negotiators can begin narrowing down the options by identifying and eliminating any non-negotiables. Once they have agreed on a short list of viable options, they can then use objective criteria to compare each one against the others. For example, if one option requires extensive renovations while another only requires minor repairs and upgrades, a buyer might choose the less expensive option even though it may not be their first choice.

Pre-negotiation strategies like these will help negotiators avoid getting locked into a particular solution and allow them to focus on finding the best possible outcome instead. When the time comes to sit down and negotiate, you should be prepared. You should have done your research on the other party and known their needs, goals, and objectives. You should also ensure you have all the facts concerning the issue at hand so you can use them as leverage during discussions.

Themes of Negotiation

Negotiation isn't just limited to a conversation about what should happen but also about how to get there. Themes can be a powerful tool for a fruitful negotiation. These themes are basically stories. By weaving together themes, you can create a story that connects people on both sides of the table. Themes represent the emotional heart of negotiation and can be used to create a memorable experience that will leave both parties feeling like they've achieved something significant. When you're crafting a theme, think about what's most important to you. Is it creating an environment where everyone feels heard? Is it getting people to work together instead of against each other? Whatever your goal is, find ways to weave that into the story so everyone knows why they're there.

The following themes are pioneered by Christopher "Chris" Voss, a former FBI negotiator and author of the best-selling book Never Split the Difference. He recommends using active listening to show that you're putting real skin into the game and understanding what the other person is saying.

Mirroring

We discussed mirroring previously, but this powerful social tool is critical anytime negotiation is at play. Mirroring is the act of subtly reflecting a person's behaviors, speech patterns, and body language back to them, and is a proven way to build rapport and create a sense of understanding. We'll take this tactic a step further in this section to unlock a higher level of active listening that gives you the ability to persuade and stay in control of a conversation with almost no effort.

Mirroring shows the other party you're listening closely to what they say and it builds trust. It also helps establish an emotional connection between both parties, which increases the likelihood that each side will feel like they've been treated fairly. When you hear something you don't like, disagree with, or are unsure of how to respond, take mirroring to a literal level. Simply repeat back a summary of the last thing the person said, but repeat it as a question.

Let's say that you're negotiating a deal with a potential client. You finish your presentation and they say something like, "I see what you're saying but I'm not sure this fully addresses the bigger picture." Your response can be as absurdly simple as: "the bigger picture?" in a neutral, inquisitive tone. By repeating this phrase back to them, you've acknowledged their concern but did not agree with it —which is crucial because it shows you're listening but not convinced by their position. What exactly is the bigger picture? You can't know that unless the client tells you. By mirroring here, you are validating the other person's concern while gaining the knowledge you can use to negotiate more effectively. The added benefit is that you have removed the spotlight from you and focused it back on the subject, gaining time to formulate a strong response.

In a simpler example, you're with a few friends after the movies and the group is indecisive about where to eat dinner. You have a place in mind and propose your favorite burger joint, but someone in the group quickly dismisses it saying, "not that place, I had a bad experience last time". You might argue your point. Maybe you deflate, dismissing your own idea. Perhaps you even try to influence the group to follow you and disregard the other person. An easier way to confront this person is to simply mirror them: "you had a bad experience?" and allow them to elaborate. It puts the spotlight on them and they must give a good reason why they shot down your idea. If their concerns are valid, you and the group can propose a restaurant that everyone enjoys. But if they were just being disagreeable, they will make your argument for you because they had to explain.

Labeling

Emotions are not barriers but the key to successful negotiation. The relationship between an emotionally intelligent negotiator and their counterpart is similar to that of a psychotherapist with their patient. Like psychotherapists, negotiators probe to understand the issues that concern their counterparts. They then use this information to formulate a strategy and get opposing parties to see things differently so that agreements can be reached. They understand that humans make decisions based on emotion, not logic.

To become more emotionally intelligent, you must learn to listen to the core of what's being said, beyond just the words someone is using to express it. Listening is one of the most powerful tools in your arsenal. This is because it allows you to understand what makes your counterpart tick and how they feel about a situation. It also helps you gauge where the common ground exists between the two of you. Keep this in mind as you speak, too. Try to use words that describe the root of what you are communicating.

Emotions can flair up in negotiation, pushing the conversation off course or erasing the common ground that had been established. When this happens, maintain control by addressing (labeling) the emotion rather than bulldozing it. This validates the feeling the other person is expressing and diffuses the situation to a degree by putting it front and center in the conversation. Instead of returning anger with a raised voice, say something like "it sounds like you're in a bind here, and that must be frustrating," and ask to explore that frustration further. Make sure the other person feels heard, and respond directly to the issue they present rather than the emotion they display. It may sound like you're supposed to submit to your counterpart, but this tactic does the opposite. By maintaining control over your emotions and labeling how you observe your counterpart to be behaving, you demonstrate that you are stable, trustworthy, and confident.

You shouldn't criticize or judge your counterpart's actions but instead, focus on understanding why they did what they did. For instance, if they fail to deliver their part of the project on time, don't start blaming them for being lazy or disorganized. Instead, try asking questions like "what led up to this situation?" or "how do we ensure that it never happens again?" The most important thing is that you should never make any assumptions about your counterpart's motivations, and instead try to get them to explain their actions.

Tactical Empathy

Negotiations break down when the parties involved feel as though their concerns are not being heard. Dealing with a tough negotiation by pretending to be obtuse or ignoring the other party's position will only frustrate that person and make them less likely to do what you want. Some people can get away with being a tough negotiator, but this is rarely the best way to comc to an agreement.

Tactical empathy is the ability to recognize, understand, and respond effectively to another person's position. You can enhance your relationship with them for a successful negotiation by effectively summarizing their pain points back to them when the time is right. Listen to what they are telling you, observe what they might not be sharing, and ask clarifying questions throughout the negotiation. Mirroring can gain you key insights, and labeling should keep them comfortable and willing to continue sharing more with you.

Once you feel like you have walked in the other person's shoes long enough to adequately understand where they are coming from, tell them what you have learned. If you are truly on the same page, they will respond extremely positively to your summary. If not, you have given them a chance to correct you. The goal of tactical empathy is to prove you not only understand the other party's situation, but you know how they feel about it, too.

Bend the Rules

Negotiation is a complex, dynamic process: every negotiation has its own unique set of variables. It's important to understand that there is no such thing as a set of rules that apply in every negotiation. The key is to learn what works best for you and your situation. Some of the tactics above may seem unnatural at first. You can always start small, and I would suggest starting with the mirroring technique. Simply repeat a phrase back to someone in the form of a question and sit back as they elaborate freely on whatever they were discussing. You'll be shocked by how much information a bit of innocent mirroring can bring out from someone.

Once you learn to read the unspoken language of needs and expectations, you can master a universe of variables that will enable you to change your counterpart's thinking. For instance, if your counterpart is demanding a certain price and you know they really need to make this sale, then you can use that need to your advantage. You can say something like, "I understand that you're selling this car for a good price because it has very low mileage, but if we can work out an arrangement where I pay $20 less per week, would that make it more appealing?" You're not asking for a discount; you're just asking for a lower payment. This is an example of how to use the unspoken language of needs and expectations to get what you want.

When you ask for something, make sure that it's something that they can actually deliver. You don't want to waste your time negotiating if there is no chance of success.

Reinforce Positive Emotions

When you start a negotiation, it's crucial that you don't come across as aggressive or confrontational. You want to be seen as someone willing to work together with the other person rather than against them. One way to diffuse a negative situation is by addressing it head-on without judgment. Labeling a negative can help diffuse its power over you and those around you if you focus on the result rather than the behavior.

Say you're working with colleagues on a project and one of the team consistently shoots down ideas and offers minimal solutions. One response to this could be "why are you always so negative?" which puts that person in the hot seat and likely puts the whole group on edge. A negative label, such as "It seems like you want this project to fail," can highlight the problem and call into question the motivation for that person's behavior. You have moved beyond the negative emotion and focused on the negotiation at hand. The person behaving negatively is unlikely to feel personally attacked by this type of statement, and you have labeled what seems like a desire to fail. Once someone realizes they appear to be sabotaging the project, they are likely to contribute in positive ways to mend their image.

Key Takeaways

- Negotiation is merely another form of communication and, as such, relies on proper listening skills and assertiveness.
- Effective negotiation also requires understanding your needs, wants, and limits. Always take time to reflect on them before a negotiation begins.
- Negotiation isn't just limited to business settings. If you view difficult conversations with friends, family members, and romantic partners as negotiations, and apply effective negotiation tactics to them, you will have more productive conversations by diffusing emotional barriers.
- Often, you'll have to bend the rules of negotiation to get what you want; but if you're not willing to do this, be prepared to accept whatever terms your counterpart offers.
- It's important to know that negotiation is a skill, and like any other skill, it can be learned. If you're not confident in your ability to negotiate effectively, practice with friends and family members when the stakes are low.

Remember that negotiation is a two-way street. It's important to listen closely to what your counterpart has to say because there are often items on the agenda that will benefit you as well. If you can't find common ground on all issues, try to compromise on those with which you disagree. Don't focus on one issue too much. Remain flexible in your thinking and address disagreements candidly. Everything does not need to be solved in one conversation. By setting goals before any conversation that features negotiation, you can determine small victories and help not to get bogged down in ugly details. This can help both parties get a fresh perspective on the issues at hand.

The next chapter will teach you how to apply these techniques in more casual conversations and show you how easy it is to take control of a conversation once you understand this basic principle.

Chapter 10
Difficult Conversations with Family and Loved Ones

"A lot of problems in the world would be solved if we talked to each other instead of about each other."

— Nickey Gumble

Comprehension in relationships is a critical component that requires practice and patience. Sometimes you must be the one to take the first step if you want to alter a relationship with someone very close to you. Look beyond your thoughts and emotions to understand what they're trying to say.

Everyone wants to be understood and seen. Consequently, your interpersonal interactions will flourish if you actively work to make those around you feel heard and noticed. By doing so, you will be able to connect with your loved ones more effectively and allow everyone in your life to be their best selves.

There are situations when a serious conversation is needed, and if you struggle to communicate with ease, this may be daunting. This chapter will cover how to prepare and deliver your message in a stressful situation. It always pays to be prepared, so we will also cover what to do when your conversation doesn't go over as well as you might have hoped.

Preparing for Conversation as a Way to Communicate Effectively

To understand your loved ones, you need to have effective and engaging conversations. These can be difficult depending on how much effort you are willing to put in.

Here are some strategies to get you ready for a tough conversation:

Note Your Ideas

Write down your intended message before starting a conversation. What emotions do you feel? What is the most effective way to express your truth? Consider your goals as well. Are you looking for a resolution or clarification? Are you only attempting to let go of suppressed feelings and emotions? What result are you aiming to achieve by addressing this issue? By organizing your thoughts, the goal will become clear, and a focus will emerge, directing your words in the right pattern.

Breathe in Deeply

Give yourself a chance to breathe. Slowly exhale after taking a deep breath. Your entire body should be at ease. Breathing slowly relaxes your parasympathetic nervous system allowing your muscles to relax and deflate. If you have some time before the conversation, you can also unwind by listening to some music.

Evoke Empathy

Try to put yourself in the shoes of the other person. Every story has two points of view. There are reasons why people behave the way they do. Perhaps they were raised in a family with strong values different from yours. Perhaps they have difficulty connecting and being vulnerable. Knowing the motivations behind someone's behavior may encourage compassion. Everyone involved will benefit if the other person feels less overwhelmed due to empathy and acceptance.

Clear Your Anticipations and Expectations

Bring no preconceived notions to the conversation. If your expectations are not met, disappointment, despair, and irritability may rear their ugly heads. Allow the conversation to develop naturally rather than expecting an apology, a specific response, or comfort from the other party. Accept it for what it is at that precise moment.

Emanate a Positive Vibe

You're not going into a nice conversation, so this might be difficult. Try to focus on the desired outcome and how great it will feel to get this off your chest. Focus on how much you love the person you are confronting, and the peace you will gain once you have asserted yourself and cleared this up.

How to Pass Your Message Across Clearly

You can't communicate effectively if you struggle to convey a message. Below you'll find several tips for delivering a clear message and reducing friction and misunderstanding as much as possible.

Here are some ideas for getting your message across clearly:

Don't Deviate from the Message

Make sure that the person or group you are speaking to understands the ideas you are attempting to convey. What do you want them to understand the most? How do you want them to interpret the message? Leave nothing up to the guesswork of your listener.

Create a Two-Way Dialogue

Make an effort to hear and comprehend the perspectives of others. What do they hope to convey? Which signals are they attempting to communicate to you? Take note of what they say and don't say through gestures and body language.

Be Concise

Focus on objective truths where possible and get right to the point. When honesty is combined with discretion, it produces the best results. Consider how what you're about to say will affect the other person or people. Think twice about its relevancy before choosing to reveal an unpleasant truth or your interpretation of events. Express how the situation makes you feel; not your full interpretation of the situation.

Respect Your Audience

You must first understand that your message is not solely about you or your desires. The key concept is to consider what is truly in it for your listener/audience. If you want to be heard, you must believe in your argument and show genuine concern for your listener's wants and specific points of view. It is critical to recognize and respect the fact that each of us has a unique perspective based on our circumstances, motivations, and needs.

Eliminate Weak and Vague Words

Make your sentences as precise and straightforward as possible. Avoid filler words and ones that make you sound weak or unsure, like "kind of" and "sort of."

Use Nonverbal Communication Techniques

Body language, or nonverbal cues, can be used to convey feelings and intentions. Humans can pick up on unspoken emotions by reading and understanding other people's body language.

There are a few occasions when, despite your best efforts, you find yourself in a heated argument or tense situation with the individual. This is not a failure; you simply need to know what steps to take to de-escalate the tension.

How to De-Escalate Tension

Conversations with loved ones can sometimes spiral out of control due to heightened emotions and the discussion of past transgressions. Even with the best intentions, broaching sensitive topics with family can bring tense emotions and toxic behavior to the surface.

It is critical to understand how to de-escalate tension:

Control Your Feelings

Approach the other person calmly. To begin, take a moment to collect your thoughts, breathe deeply, and remind yourself of your goals. If the situation worsens, avoid reacting angrily or rashly. Never respond immediately and give yourself a few seconds to think before speaking.

Recognize the Other Person's Emotions

Simply pay attention and acknowledge the listener's emotions. Avoid attempting to solve or fix the problem, and do not consider whether they are right or wrong. You can validate their emotions but you are the one in charge of the conversation, so don't allow the other person to derail the conversation. People who are angry lack the cognitive ability to think critically. Switching to problem-solving mode will be ineffective and may worsen the situation.

Stay Present and Don't Leave the Scene Unless Necessary

Walking away is a passive-aggressive behavior that will escalate the situation because the other person may feel ignored or mistreated. You should only leave if you are unable to control yourself or feel threatened in any way. Otherwise, stay put, express your support, keep your emotions in check, and stick to your message.

Demonstrate Proper Self-Discipline and Emotional Control

This is critical to maintaining control of the situation. When the angry person sees your calm and considerate behavior, they feel pressured to correct themselves. Social norms do not reward anger in any situation, and when a person is unable to manage their anger, they are viewed as out of control. The upset individual will follow your lead, and you can now redirect the conversation. That will allow you to identify the factors that contributed to the escalation, clear up any misunderstandings or miscommunications, and brainstorm solutions together.

Setting Boundaries and Redirecting the Conversation

Changing the subject in the middle of a conversation is a separate art form that must be mastered. No matter how gracefully you can pivot, some topics come up several times and you may not be in the right frame of mind to discuss them. To avoid conflict, you may need to quickly change the direction of the conversation. This is where setting bound-aries comes into play.

Here are some pointers on how to set your boundaries and politely change the subject:

Set Boundaries to Focus

You began this conversation focused on one issue. Let's say the listener repeatedly brings a separate issue to the table. This is manipulative behavior, whether it is being done intentionally or not. You have the right to establish a boundary around that issue for the time being so you can focus on the conversation at hand.

Don't Wait Until You Can't Take It

This takes courage and practice, but the earlier you mention these boundaries in a conversation, the better.

You may anticipate certain conflicts, so it could be best to get ahead of any interruption to your focus topic by establishing boundaries right off the bat.

Our boundaries aren't always respected, and this can be especially frustrating when dealing with loved ones. When your boundaries aren't respected, you'll have to deal with this specific type of invalidation.

How to Deal with Invalidation in a Family Setting

Handling invalidation with maturity necessitates self-assurance and trust.

The following are practical steps to help you deal with invalidation from a loved one or in a familial setting:

Start by Validating Yourself

Many people become trapped because they believe they require others to authenticate their emotions. They think that for a relationship to be fulfilling, they must be intimately understood by someone. This is especially pronounced in strained familial relationships. We will go to great lengths in an attempt to be fully understood by someone who may not have the capacity or the desire to see what we are trying to communicate.

The reality is you don't need anyone – not even your family, spouse, or partner - to confirm your feelings are valid. What matters is the fact that you recognize that your beliefs are genuine. Nobody can authenticate your emotions besides you. External validation is useless until you can provide it for yourself.

Being compassionate with yourself is essential. Regardless of what others think or say about you, remind yourself that you are valuable and that you matter. This understanding and conviction can be extremely effective in dealing with invalidators. You deserve to take up space just as much as anyone else.

Confront the Invalidator

This is a difficult step because the invalidator may or may not be aware of how their behavior is affecting you. You are not in it to start a fight; this should be a cool-headed conversation about how you feel. It is critical to clarify matters, especially if the person is a loved one. The person might be willing and able to change their behavior, or you may need to set some firm boundaries that limits their presence in your life.

Expect Discontentment from the Invalidator

A common reaction to a confrontation is more invalidation, especially from those who intended to invalidate your emotions or ideas in the first place. They may ignore or exaggerate your claim. Depending on the individual, you may be able to find common ground. The confrontation may also result in dissatisfaction and insults from the invalidator.

This is why it is not enough to know how to deal with invalidation; it is also necessary to know how to deal with insults.

How to Handle Insults

We can't always avoid negative or disrespectful people. What matters is what you do when you are forced to deal with them.

The following are some ways to deal with insults:

Keep Your Cool and Control Your Anger

When you are insulted, you naturally become agitated and angry. This is a poor response to insults because it implies that you accept the insult, which is the primary goal of the assaulter. You have validated their negativity and given it a place at the table. Consequently, if you are insulted, you should first remain composed, calm, and relaxed. Don't respond right away and keep your wits about you. Recognize the insult as a dirty tactic meant to make you angry - and try not to give in.

Respond Politely or Ignore

After you've paused, you might decide to respond to the insult, or you may simply ignore it. One way to respond to an insult is to make a lighthearted joke to relieve tension while not shying away. You could change the subject or assertively state the conversation needs to move on. You may also choose to address the issue, particularly if the person is close to you. Allow them to understand how you feel about their statement.

To ignore an insult is to invite it back, stronger and more piercing than before. Sometimes it is senseless to give attention to a superficial matter but pay attention to the intent of the other person. Ignoring a knee-jerk rude comment is fine sometimes, but insults that come from a deeper disrespect or intimate knowledge between two people must be addressed.

Stay Focused

You may have scratched the surface of a delicate matter by confronting someone who invalidates you. When people are uncomfortable in a conversation, they will seek to derail it by any means. This could result in insulting language and dismissive or aggressive behavior. Shift focus from their insult back to the conversation, do not allow them to change its course. It's easy to get caught up in a response to an insult, but stay focused on your reason for bringing the topic up in the first place. This is always easier when you have prepared for the conversation beforehand.

Cool Off

Sometimes an insulting conversation doesn't have a smooth ending. If someone is intent on hurling insults or invalidating you and is not willing to change their behavior, you need to end the conversation. As we discussed previously, effective communication cannot be a one-sided endeavor. You cannot fix the other person's behavior, so you need to shelf the conversation until they are able to contribute equally.

Key Takeaways

Preparing for Conversation as a Way to Communicate Effectively

- Jot notes of your ideas and feelings
- Write down your goals for the conversation

- Breathe in deeply
- Evoke empathy
- Clear your anticipations and expectations

How to Clearly Get Your Message Across

- Create a two-way dialogue
- Be concise
- Respect your audience
- Eliminate weak and vague words
- Use strong nonverbal communication techniques

How to De-escalate Tension

- Control your feelings
- Recognize the other person's emotions
- Demonstrate self-discipline and emotional control

Setting Boundaries and Redirecting the Conversation

- Stay focused
- Don't wait till you can't take it

How to Deal with Invalidation

- Start by validating yourself
- Confront the invalidator
- Expect the invalidator to be discontent

How to Handle Insults

- Keep your cool and control your anger
- Respond politely or ignore

Relationships are essential to human existence and can only be maintained through effective communication. It's not always easy, but difficult conversations are the ones from which we stand to gain the most.

Chapter 11
Speak Your Mind... Forever

---

*"When you give yourself permission to communi-
cate what matters to you in every situation, you will
have peace despite rejection or disapproval. Putting
a voice to your soul helps you to let go of the negative
energy of fear and regret."*

— Shannon L. Alder

When I was younger, I was always told to "speak my mind."
As I got older, I realized we all need a bit of a filter and
adapt to our environment. After all, not everyone wants to
hear what I have to say! It seems like everywhere you look,
people are telling you to "watch what you say." Whether it's
in the workplace or on social media, there's a lot of pressure
to censor yourself. What happens when you bite your
tongue for too long?

Why Should You Speak Your Mind

1. Helps You Express Your True Feelings

First, speaking your mind allows you to express yourself fully. When you hold your opinion back, you're not being true to yourself. While it's important to be respectful of others, you shouldn't have to diminish your importance to do so.

It's important to be able to speak your mind freely. The ability to express yourself without fear of reprisal is critical to mental and emotional health. When you're able to freely share your thoughts and feelings, you're more likely to cope with stress in a healthy way, build strong relationships, and make better decisions. People who bottle up their emotions are more likely to suffer from anxiety and depression. In addition, NCBI research has shown that employees who don't feel comfortable speaking up about problems at work are more likely to experience job-related stress and burnout. When you're able to openly communicate your needs and concerns, you're more likely to feel supported and empowered. Consequently, it's essential to create an environment in which you feel safe to speak your mind.

2. Helps You Understand Your Beliefs

Secondly, speaking your mind can help you better understand and refine your own beliefs. It's easy to say you believe something, but it's another thing entirely to be able to explain why you believe it. You can think about why you believe what you do, and you can explore the evidence that supports your beliefs. This process of self-examination can be uncomfortable, but it is essential for understanding your values and determining which beliefs are worth holding on to. In addition, speaking your mind also allows you to confront opposing viewpoints. This can be challenging, but it is a necessary part of developing a well-rounded perspective. By considering different points of view, you can gain a deeper understanding of the issues at hand and learn to approach problems from multiple angles. Ultimately, speaking your mind is essential for understanding your beliefs and expanding your worldview.

3. Helps in Changing People's Perspectives Persuade Others / Get your way

Thirdly, speaking your mind can also help change the minds of others. If everyone always agreed with each other, there would be no progress. It's only by sharing different perspectives and learning from each other that humanity can hope to move forward. Many people find it difficult to speak their minds, especially when they are in the minority. This is because they worry about being ridiculed or rejected by the majority. However, research by Helen Fields suggests that speaking your mind can also help to change the minds of others. In a study published in the journal Social Psychology, participants were asked to read about a controversial issue, such as gun control or abortion. They were then asked to state their opinions on the issue, either privately or publicly. The results showed that those who spoke their minds publicly were more likely to change the minds of others than those who stated their opinions privately. The researchers believe that this is because speaking your mind publicly allows you to present your arguments clearly and persuasively. Going public also shows that you are confident in your own beliefs, which can make others more open to reconsidering their own positions. Next time you find yourself in a minority opinion, don't be afraid to speak up. You may just change some minds in the process.

Whenever you're tempted to stay silent on a controversial issue, remember that speaking your mind is important for both you and society as a whole. Be respectful, thoughtful, and inquisitive, and most importantly, speak only what you know to be true.

How Can You Continue Speaking Your Mind?

1. Maintain Your Composure

There are times when you need to do so in a calm, collected way - especially if the issue at hand is a sensitive one. Maintaining your composure during these conversations can be difficult, but it's crucial if you want to be heard and respected. Here are a few tips on how to do just that.

One of the most important things to remember is to stay calm. This can be difficult if you're feeling passionate about the issue, but it's crucial that you remain level-headed. If you start raising your voice or getting agitated, the other person is likely to tune you out or become defensive. Speak slowly and deliberately, and take a few deep breaths if you need to.

It's also important to be respectful, even if you don't agree with the other person. Avoid personal attacks or name-calling and try to see their point of view - even if you don't agree with it. Listen carefully to what they're saying and respond thoughtfully. If the conversation starts to get heated, take a step back and try to reframe the issue more constructively.

Finally, remember that it's okay to disagree. Healthy debates can be beneficial - as long as they're conducted respectfully. Don't be afraid to share your opinion, even if it differs from someone else's. Just make sure you do so in a way that keeps everyone involved in the conversation calm and respectful. Focus on the issue rather than the person.

2. Find Your People

It's no secret that many of us find it difficult to speak up and share our opinions. No one fits in everywhere. Whether we're afraid of being judged, rejected, or simply don't know how to express ourselves, there are several reasons why we might keep quiet. However, it's important to remember that your voice is meant to be heard.

If certain topics are particularly difficult for you to discuss, start by discussing them with someone supportive and understanding. Once you feel more comfortable talking about these topics out loud, you'll find it easier to share your thoughts with others.

Some of the techniques mentioned in this book may seem uncomfortable or impossible to employ. You may not be able to imagine yourself using a negotiation tactic like mirroring or labeling and appearing natural. Try some of these things out with people you're close to and whose feedback you would welcome.

3. Use an Assertive Tone

Assertiveness is a delicate behavior to advocate since many inconsiderate and aggressive people excel at asserting themselves. You don't want to come across as abrasive or insensitive. If you're never assertive, you will never be able to get all you want from life. Opportunities will pass you by because no one knew you were interested. People will take advantage of you because they never knew about your boundaries. You may end up feeling resentful and powerless.

How can you strike the right balance? The key is that your assertiveness should come from the point of view that you are no less important, and no more important than the person you are speaking to. Your needs and wants are of equal value.

Use an assertive tone of voice. This never means yelling or being aggressive; it means communicating clearly and confidently, keeping control of any negative emotions. When you do this, people are more likely to listen to what you have to say. They'll also be more likely to respect your opinions and boundaries.

If you're not sure how to speak up assertively, start by practicing in low-stakes situations. For example, try expressing your opinions during a casual conversation with friends or family members. Once you feel more confident, start speaking up in more challenging situations, such as at work or during a heated discussion with a loved one. Remember, the goal is not to win every argument; it's simply to express yourself honestly and confidently.

4. Exude Confidence (even if you don't feel confident)

It's no secret that confidence is key in almost every aspect of life. Whether you're trying to impress your boss, land a date, or make new friends, exuding confidence can help you achieve your goals. But what happens when you're not feeling confident? How can you fake it until you make it?

Here are a few tips:

- Stand up straight and make eye contact. Good posture and direct eye contact convey confidence and show that you're not intimidated by others.
- Speak slowly and clearly. Rushing your words or mumbling can make you seem nervous or uncertain. Take your time and enunciate clearly to project confidence.
- Avoid "upspeak." You probably know what I'm talking about--ending your sentences with a higher pitch as if you're asking a question even when you're not. This habit makes you sound unsure of yourself, so try to avoid it.
- Use strong language. Words like "absolutely," and "definitely," convey conviction and certainty. Choose your words carefully to come across as confident, even if you don't feel that way.
- Be prepared. If you walk into a situation knowing what you're doing, you'll automatically feel more confident than if you're winging it. Do your research, practice ahead of time, and go into whatever it is feeling prepared and ready to succeed.
- Less is more. Brevity comes off as witty, intelligent, and thoughtful.

These are just a few tips on how to appear more confident. Just remember: faking confidence is often half the battle. Once you act the part, the rest will follow suit.

5. Don't Worry About What Other People May Think

In today's world, it's easy to get caught up in what others think of you. With social media, it's easy to compare yourself to others and feel like you're not good enough. However, it's important to remember that you are your own person with your own unique talents and qualities. It's important to speak your mind and be true to yourself. Be confident in who you are, even if you're still figuring that out. Don't let anyone else control your life. You're the only one making decisions that will make you happy. Live your life the way you want to, and don't let anyone else tell you how to live it.

6. Practice Speaking Your Mind in Low-Stake Conversation

It can be difficult to speak your mind, especially when you're not used to it. It's important to practice so that you can do it more easily in high-stakes situations. Here are some tips for practicing speaking your mind in low-stakes conversations:

- Choose a safe environment. Pick a situation where you feel comfortable speaking up. This could be with a friend or family member or in a small group setting.
- Start small. Begin by saying something simple, like "I would rather go here than there." Or "I see where you're coming from but I see that very differently."

- Be assertive, not aggressive. Make sure your tone is respectful and confident, not confrontational or defensive.
- Listen and respond thoughtfully. When the other person responds to what you've said, take the time to listen to their point of view and respond accordingly. Don't just emotionally.
- Keep practicing. The more you do it, the easier it will become. Don't be afraid to speak up next time you're in a conversation!

How to Know When to Speak Up

1.   Contribute   Towards   Enlightening Discussions

It's important to know when to speak up and when to stay silent. You don't want to be the person who incessantly talks just for the sake of talking, but you also don't want to fade into the background. How can you strike the perfect balance? Enlightening discussions can come from differing viewpoints. Don't shy away from disagreeing, but make sure that your comments are backed up with examples or scenarios. Preface opinionated comments with phrases like "I think..." or "I believe that...". This will show that you're open to other points of view and that you're willing to engage in respectful discourse. By following these simple guidelines, you'll soon become known as a valuable member of any conversation.

2. Decision-Making Process

If people never speak up in a group, it doesn't mean that they don't have any strong opinions. They tend to think things through carefully before voicing their opinion, and as a result, they usually know what they want to say by the time the conversation gets around to them. That said, there are definitely times when it's important to speak up sooner rather than later. For example, if you're involved in a decision-making process, make sure you share your thoughts and preferences early on. That way, everyone can consider your point of view, and you can reach a decision that works for everyone. Try something like "Do you think it would work better if we..." or "What if instead of going to the stadium, we curl up and watch the match on the couch?" In general, then, it's important to speak up when you have something valuable to add to the discussion – regardless of whether you're the first person to do so.

3. When Your Silence Is Mistaken for Approval

When we stay quiet in the face of bad behavior, we give the impression that we approve of it. For example, if I see a man making lewd comments to a woman, my silence might be interpreted as a sign that I think his behavior is acceptable. In situations like this, it is important to speak up and let the person know that their behavior is not welcome. This can be done in a firm but respectful way by saying something like, "What makes you think it's acceptable to behave that way?" By speaking up, we send the message that we will not tolerate bad behavior and that we stand with those who are being mistreated.

Improving Communication Skills is a Lifelong Endeavor

Most people would agree that communication is essential to our daily lives. Whether we're communicating with our family, friends, or colleagues, the ability to express ourselves clearly and effectively is crucial to maintaining relationships and getting our needs met. Unfortunately, many of us find communication to be a challenge. If you're struggling with your communication skills, don't despair - there are plenty of ways to improve and I hope this book has been a helpful step in the right direction.

One of the first steps to improving communication is to become aware of your own style. Do you tend to be shy or withdrawn in social situations? Do you have difficulty expressing your needs or asking for help? Identifying your own communication strengths and weaknesses can help you to make improvements.

Essential to better communication is learning to listen actively. This means giving full attention to the person who is speaking, making eye contact, and not interrupting. It also means trying to understand the message being communicated rather than just hearing the words. It is the opposite of simply waiting for your turn to speak. Active listening is an important skill in all human relationships.

If you're looking to improve your communication skills, remember that it's a lifelong process. By taking small steps and practicing regularly, you can gradually make progress and start enjoying more successful and satisfying relationships with the people in your life.

Take Control of the Conversation

Have you ever been in a conversation where you felt like you were just reacting, instead of driving the conversation? It can be frustrating and even draining. Luckily, there's a simple way to take control of the conversation without taking control of the other person. All you have to do is put them in the driver's seat. By asking questions and allowing them to lead the conversation, you'll find that you can still steer the conversation in the direction you want it to go without taking all the work on yourself. Not only will this make the conversation more interesting for both of you, but it will also give you a much-needed break. Next time you feel like you're stuck in a rut, try putting the other person in the driver's seat and see where the conversation takes you.

Practice, Practice, Practice..

When it comes to practicing your conversation skills, it's important to find a balance between low- and high-stakes conversations. Low-stakes conversations are those that don't have a lot riding on them - they're often practice sessions or discussions that aren't particularly important. High-stakes conversations are those that have a lot of potential conse- quences - for example, a job interview or a discussion with your boss. While it's important to practice both types of conversations, low-stakes conversations are often the best place to start. That's because they provide an opportunity to experiment and make mistakes without any real conse- quences.

There are a few different ways you can go about finding low-stakes conversations. One option is to join a group or club where the focus is on casual discussion. This could be anything from a book club to a cooking class. Another option is to set up regular coffee dates with friends or acquaintances. This gives you the chance to chat in a relaxed setting without any pressure. Finally, you can simply strike up conversations with people you meet in everyday life - for example, the cashier at your local grocery store or the person sitting next to you on the bus. By taking the time to practice your conversation skills in low-stakes situations, you'll be better prepared for when it really matters.

Key Takeaways

- It is essential to be able to freely speak your mind to fully express yourself, understand your beliefs, and change people's perspectives.
- This allows you to express yourself fully, understand your beliefs, and change the minds of others.
- You can continue speaking your mind by maintaining composure, conversing with people who make you feel at ease, using an assertive tone, sounding confident, and not worrying about what other people think.
- Practice speaking your mind in low-stakes conversations so that you can do it more easily in high-stakes situations.

Conclusion

Many people today deal with crippling social anxiety, low self-esteem, and an inability to communicate for various other reasons. There are a thousand barriers to effective communication, and dealing with them is no easy task. Nonetheless, the good news is that you've taken the first step to dealing with your communication issue and starting on this journey to improve your skills. By now, you've gained the skills and knowledge you need to talk to absolutely anybody, whether it's your boss, a romantic interest, or an estranged friend.

Hopefully, as you've gone through each chapter, you've already applied the techniques presented to better your overall communication skills. However, even if you haven't started implementing these tricks into your practical life, it's time to take action. On your journey to improvement, the next step is to practice all the techniques. After all, practice is the fountainhead of all smooth communication. Don't be under the impression that you'll turn your life around overnight after finishing this book. Only by practicing each technique will you be able to see a significant difference in your communication skills.

Remember, the secret to a good and healthy conversation is to keep an open mind to other people's opinions. Be an active listener to make people feel validated and heard. This is not only the right thing to do, but it gives you power. You'll feel them keeping an open mind when it comes to your opinions and they will be comfortable to share more with you. Take their concerns into consideration, and learn to be empathetic, but, at the same time, learn to be assertive. These two qualities should go hand in hand when you're talking to anyone. Only then will you be able to have a balanced and fruitful conversation. Many people need to understand the importance of assertiveness and how to say no. No matter how smooth of a communicator you are, you will be taken advantage of without this quality.

Furthermore, don't underestimate the significance of small talk. It may seem unnecessary at the time, but it is what leads to a real and meaningful conversation. Hopefully, you've learned how to turn small talk into active conversations by now. You'll see a real change in not just your communication style but also your attitude and personality. Developing your people skills will ultimately make you more charming, persuasive, and harder to resist.

Scan me

Scan the QR code above to claim your free bonuses

——————————— OR ———————————

https://tinyurl.com/jason-forte

Get Ready to Improve all your Conversations & Build Self-Confidence!

✔Five Simple Secrets of Great Communicators. Treat these tips as your bible to improve your communication skills.

✔Free e-book: Stop Limiting Yourself. Expert advice debunks the most common limiting beliefs and forces you to get out of your own head!

✔Printable Small-Talk Field Guide, including conversation topic inventory worksheet. Never be left with nothing to say, and learn to exit a conversation gracefully.

Thank You

Thank you for buying my book. I hope it was both informing and insightful.

Before you go, can I ask you for one small favor? **Could you please leave a review on Amazon?**

Your feedback helps independent authors like me to create more books that will hopefully keep on helping you and others.

It would mean a lot to hear from you.

References

5 types of communication styles. (n.d.). Valamis. https://www.valamis.-com/hub/communication-styles

Assertive communication. (n.d.). Gov.au. https://www.healthywa.wa.gov-.au/Articles/A_E/Assertive-communication

Blank, A. (2022, May 3). 3 steps to help you regain control over A conversation. Forbes. https://www.forbes.com/sites/averyblank/2022/05/03/3-steps-to-help-you-regain-control-over-a-conversation/

Communication skills. (2018, November 8). Corporate Finance Institute. https://corporatefinanceinstitute.com/resources/careers/soft-skills/communication/

Know your communication style and impact. (n.d.). Effective Training Associates. from https://effectivetraining.com/know-your-communica-tion-style-impact/

Swords, C. (2019, June 5). Why Self-Awareness is Crucial in your Communications. Linkedin.com. https://www.linkedin.com/pulse/why-self-awareness-crucial-your-communications-charley-swords

Use these techniques to take control of an English conversation. (2015, July 7). EF English Live. https://englishlive.cf.com/blog/study tips/use tech-niques-take-control-english-conversation/

(c) Copyright skillsyouneed.com 2011-. (n.d.). Active listening. Skillsy-ouneed.com. https://www.skillsyouneed.com/ips/active-listening.html

Cuncic, A. (2010, May 10). 7 active listening techniques to practice in your daily conversations. Verywell Mind. https://www.verywellmind.-com/what-is-active-listening-3024343

Half, R. (2022, April 13). 10 quotes to inspire active listening in the work-place. Roberthalf.com. https://www.roberthalf.com/blog/salaries-and-skills/10-quotes-to-inspire-active-listening

The science of listening. (2021, April 15). Kornferry.com; Korn Ferry. https://www.kornferry.com/insights/briefings-magazine/issue-13/514-the-science-of-listening

WomensMedia. (2012, November 9). 10 steps to effective listening. Forbes. https://www.forbes.com/sites/womensmedia/2012/11/09/10-steps-to-effective-listening/?sh=7d9e6dc38918

Harrington, C. (2021, December 27). Overcoming emotional invalidation.

Restoration Counseling of Atlanta. https://restorationcounselingatl.com/overcoming-emotional-invalidation/

Ponio, J. (2022, January 28). Ways to show empathy sincerely – our father's house soup kitchen. Our Father's House Soup Kitchen. https://ofhsoupkitchen.org/how-to-show-empathy

Rollo, A. (2021, September 24). Empathy or validation, or both? Heights Family Counseling. https://heightsfamilycounseling.com/blog/empathy-or-validation-or-both

Understanding Others Quotes (145 quotes). (2011). Goodreads.com. https://www.goodreads.com/quotes/tag/understanding-other

How to Make People Feel Seen and Heard. (2021, March 16). Posh. https://poosh.com/how-to-make-people-feel-seen-and-heard/

Active Listening: How to listen and make others feel heard. (n.d.). Groove | Workplace Mental Wellbeing Platform. https://www.groovnow.com/blog/active-listening-how-to-listen-and-make-others-feel-heard

Taylor, K. (2020, February 25). 6 Ways To Make Your Partner Feel Heard And Understood. Medium. https://psiloveyou.xyz/6-ways-to-make-your-partner-feel-heard-and-understood-482899bf57fb

Harrington, C. (2021, December 27). Overcoming Emotional Invalidation. Restoration Counseling of Atlanta. https://restorationcounselingatl.com/overcoming-emotional-invalidation/#:~:text=Ultimately%2C%20dealing%20with%20invalidation%20comes

Hofmann, S. G., Gutner, C. A., & Fang, A. (2017). Social Anxiety Disorder ☆. In Reference Module in Neuroscience and Biobehavioral Psychology. Elsevier.

National Comorbidity Survey. (n.d.). Harvard.edu. https://www.hcp.med.harvard.edu/ncs/index.php

7 tips for living with social anxiety. (n.d.). WebMD. https://www.webmd.com/anxiety-panic/tips-for-living-with-social-anxiety

Cuncic, A. (2010, August 5). Small Talk Topics. Verywell Mind. https://www.verywellmind.com/small-talk-topics-3024421

Cunnarson, V. (2015, July 10). 10 small talk tips that'll make you forget you ever had to rely on "so, how about that weather?" The Muse. https://www.themuse.com/amp/advice/10-small-talk-tips-thatll-make-you-forget-you-ever-had-to-rely-on-so-how-about-that-weather

Sivasubramaniam, J. (2018, April 3). 5 ways small talk serves a big purpose. Bkconnection.com. https://ideas.bkconnection.com/5-ways-small-talk-serves-a-big-purpose

Social anxiety disorder (social phobia). (2021, June 19). Mayo Clinic. https://www.mayoclinic.org/diseases-conditions/social-anxiety-disorder/symptoms-causes/syc-20353561

Ways to deal with awkward silences in conversations. (n.d.). Succeedsocial-ly.com. https://www.succeedsocially.com/awkwardsilences

Cohen, J. (2019, September 22). 5 reasons why People Only Text on Dating Apps. Joanncohen.com; Joann Cohen Matchmaking. https://www.joann-ncohen.com/5-reasons-why-people-only-text-on-dating-apps/

Eddie. (2022, October 1). Online dating messaging, chat, conversation tips & etiquette. San Francisco Photographer: Headshots, Portraits, Datin Coach | Headshots, Portraits & Lifestyle Photography | Dating Coach For Men, Women; Eddie Hernandez | San Francisco Bay Area Photog-rapher & Dating Coach. https://eddie-hernandez.com/online-dating-messaging-tips-and-etiquette/

Gordon, S. (2019, September 6). Understanding the dynamics of texting in relationships. Verywell Mind. https://www.verywellmind.com/under-standing-the-dynamics-of-texting-in-relationships-4769077

Lampen, C. (2018, August 17). How texting affects your relationship, according to science. Bustle. https://www.bustle.com/p/how-texting-affects-your-relationship-according-to-science-10063894

The Oracles. (2019, August 1). How to write an email that will actually get a response, according to 5 self-made millionaires. CNBC. https://www.c-nbc.com/2019/08/01/how-guarantee-an-email-response-according-to-5-self-made-millionaires.html

Walker, S. (2019, February 8). 7 benefits of texting for business communica-tion. NMS. https://newmediaservices.com.au/7-benefits-of-text-messag-ing for businesses/

Waters, S. (n.d.). How to make a good first impression: Expert tips and tricks. Betterup.com. https://www.betterup.com/blog/how-to-make-a-good-first-impression

Kelly, J. (2022, June 27). How to make A great first impression in an inter-view. Forbes. https://www.forbes.com/sites/jackkel-ly/2022/06/27/how-to-make-a-great-first-impression-in-an-interview/?sh=5b209aab594b

Bridestory. (2016, February 23). How to make a great impression on your future in-laws. Bridestory. https://www.bridestory.com/blog/how-to-make-a-great-impression-on-your-future-in-laws

Inc.Africa. (n.d.). Incafrica.com. https://incafrica.com/library/young-entrepreneur-council-8-proven-ways-to-make-a-great-first-impression-in-business

Creating a strong first impression on potential clients. (2021, September 14). BOSS Magazine; The BOSS Magazine. https://thebossmagazine.-com/creating-strong-first-impression/

Van Edwards, V. (2015, August 7). Mirroring body language: 4 steps to successfully mirror others. Science of People. https://www.scienceof-people.com/mirroring/

Baker, K. (2020b, January 7). 7 proven ways to know your audience better. HubSpot. https://blog.hubspot.com/service/know-your-audience

Mba, P. D. C. (2016, August 17). 9 tips for quickly building rapport with your audience. Linkedin.com. https://www.linkedin.com/pulse/9-tips-quickly-building-rapport-your-audience-peter-dhu-mba-csp

Boldnew. (2020, October 15). How to effectively listen to dissenting opinions in the workplace. Management Training Institute. https://manage-menttraininginstitute.com/how-to-effectively-listen-to-dissenting-opinions-in-the-workplace/

Zust, C. (n.d.). When Delivering a presentation, Look at Both Sides of nonverbal language. Kent.edu. https://www.kent.edu/yourtrainingpart-ner/when-delivering-presentation-look-both-sides-nonverbal-language

Curtis, G. (2007, February 1). How to master the art of negotiation. Investopedia website: https://www.investopedia.com/articles/pf/07/negotia-tion_tips.asp

Guadalupe, R. (2021, April 20). Take control of your negotiation using active listening techniques. Campolo, Middleton & McCormick, LLP website: https://cmmllp.com/take-control-of-your-negotiation-using-active-listening-techniques/

Scarlett, A. (2020, December 14). The Art of negotiation (Chris Voss): Summary & review. Power DynamicsTM website: https://thepower-moves.com/the-art-of-negotiation/

Shonk, K. (2022, September 26). Principled negotiation: Focus on interests to create value. PON - Program on Negotiation at Harvard Law School website: https://www.pon.harvard.edu/daily/negotiation-skills-daily/principled-negotiation-focus-interests-create-value/

Zambrano, J. C. (2022, June 18). Never split the difference by Chris Voss. from Linkedin.com website: https://www.linkedin.com/pulse/never-split-difference-chris-voss-juan-carlos-zambrano/

Foroux, D. (2020, June 12). The benefits of speaking your mind. Stoic Letter. https://medium.com/darius-foroux/the-benefits-of-speaking-your-mind-c3aea5e8dbc6

Frost, A. (2019, July 24). The ultimate guide to small talk: Conversation starters, powerful questions, & more. HubSpot. https://blog.hubspot.-com/sales/small-talk-guide

James, C. (2021, November 17). Why communication skills development is A lifelong learning journey. Master Public Speaking & Presentation Skills | CJM Training. https://colinjamesmethod.com/communication-skills-development-is-lifelong-learning/